PENGUIN BOOKS
THE CHICKEN COOKBOOK

Mrs Sharda Pargal was born in Lahore in 1936. Her father Justice Mehr Chand Mahajan was a leading lawyer of the Punjab High Court at the time, and she grew up in a profoundly nationalistic and politically aware family. She spent her early childhood in Lahore, but her formal education was in Delhi, where the family moved after partition. She completed her schooling at Lady Irwin School and graduated with a Bachelors degree in History Honours from Miranda House College.

A couple of years after her marriage she accompanied her husband to the UK where she developed her lifelong interest in the art of cooking. She experimented with Western and Chinese food and on her return to Mumbai in 1968, she started teaching Chinese, Continental and Mughlai cuisine through her pioneering cooking classes. Since then her repertoire has expanded to include Thai, Lebanese, Italian and Mexican cuisine, and it continues to evolve with the changing cosmopolitan profile of the city.

Celebrities from every walk of life, film stars and their wives, professional women and brides-in-waiting, have all been her students. She has been featured on television shows and in women's magazines and has helped several social and charitable causes.

Sharda Pargal lives in Mumbai with her husband and two daughters.

THE
CHICKEN
COOKBOOK

Sharda Pargal

PENGUIN BOOKS

PENGUIN BOOKS
Published by the Penguin Group
Penguin Books India Pvt Ltd, 11 Community Centre, Panchsheel Park, New Delhi
110 017, India
Penguin Group (USA) Inc., 375 Hudson Street, New York, New York 10014, USA
Penguin Group (Canada), 90 Eglinton Avenue East, Suite 700, Toronto, Ontario,
M4P 2Y3, Canada (a division of Pearson Penguin Canada Inc.)
Penguin Books Ltd, 80 Strand, London WC2R 0RL, England
Penguin Ireland, 25 St Stephen's Green, Dublin 2, Ireland (a division of Penguin Books
Ltd)
Penguin Group (Australia), 250 Camberwell Road, Camberwell, Victoria 3124,
Australia (a division of Pearson Australia Group Pty Ltd)
Penguin Group (NZ), cnr Airborne and Rosedale Road, Albany, Auckland 1310,
New Zealand (a division of Pearson New Zealand Ltd)
Penguin Group (South Africa) (Pty) Ltd, 24 Sturdee Avenue, Rosebank, Johannesburg
2196, South Africa

Penguin Books Ltd, Registered Offices: 80 Strand, London WC2R 0RL, England

First published by Penguin Books India 2001

Copyright © Sharda Pargal 2001

10 9 8 7 6 5 4

Typeset in Sabon by Mantra Virtual Services, New Delhi
Printed at Chaman Offset Printers, New Delhi

This book is dedicated to my parents, late Chief Justice of India, Mr Mehr Chand Mahajan and late Mrs Vidyavati Mahajan, who have enriched my life with all the beautiful colours of the world.

Contents

Contents

Acknowledgements

My husband, Virendra Pargal, has been my pillar of strength. His unconditional support, guidance and appreciation, and unstinting encouragement have made this book possible.

My best critics and admirers have been my daughters, Dr Anisha Pargal and Anjali Forbes, and my sister Rama Tandon.

My grateful thanks to my enthusiastic friend Gudoo Kapoor, who has been a great help in the compilation of this book, and to my friends Monica Sethi and Manjul Kumar who provided unwavering moral support in the initial years of my career.

I take this opportunity to thank my brothers, Jeet, Vikram, Prabodh and Yogi Mahajan; my good friend Mrs Mirdula Bhaskar; my sister-in-law Mrs Monica Mahajan; and my nieces Triveni Mahajan and Richa Bhaskar, who have supported all my endeavours over the years.

My very special thanks to Mr Khushwant Singh who introduced me to Penguin Books, Mrs Bhicoo Manekshaw who reposed faith and confidence in my expertise and Ms

V.K. Karthika for her valuable guidance.

Last but not least, my grateful thanks to Sherna Wadia for her efficient editing, patience, co-operation and valuable suggestions.

Introduction

The Indian jungle fowl is the acknowledged progenitor of domestic fowls the world over. It is native to a wide region all the way from Kashmir to Cambodïa, with perhaps the centre of its origin being in the Malaysian landmass.

From literary evidence, it appears that traditionally, non-vegetarian food was mainly meat based, and fowl is only sporadically mentioned. Ibn Batuta tells us that murgh kabab and dojaj or pulao with murgh musallam—roasted chicken or quail placed on a dish of rice cooked in ghee—were some of the items that figured on the menu during the Sultanate period. Abu Fazal in *Ain-I-Akbari* mentions that musamman—a fowl stuffed with minced meat and spices—was served at Emperor Akbar's royal court. Domingo Paes remarked on 'poultry fowls (being) remarkably cheap' in Vijayanagar. Since good beef was unavailable or scarce during colonial times, the domestic fowl was a great standby.

According to K.T. Achaya in *The Historical Dictionary of Indian Food*, the people of pre-Aryan times had no reservation in eating the karugu or kozhi (chicken), as reflected in Sangam literature. The domestic chicken made its way around the world at an early date. Magellan, the first European to reach Brazil, described how he had laid in a supply of chicken on board, in AD 1519.

Non-vegetarian food has thus been cooked, enjoyed and relished in every corner of India, since ancient times. The cuisine has been enriched by variations, which have been constantly incorporated, and have become traditional family recipes. Indian cuisine has always been as diverse as its religions, culture and regions—from Kashmir to Kanya Kumari and the Bay of Bengal to the Arabian Sea.

The shimmering snowy peaks, tall fir and poplar trees, the gurgling rivulets, and abundant fruit are God's gift to the people of Kashmir. Their exotic cuisine is laced with saffron and other aromatic herbs such as aniseed, fenugreek, ginger, asafoetida, red chillies, almonds, walnuts, sultanas, and poppy seeds. The Hindus and Muslims use different spices. The Muslims use garlic and Kashmiri onions called praan in their preparations, and lamb is the popular meat. The royal chefs of the Hindu rajas incorporated these ingredients into their own food to create delicious dishes like yakhani gosht, meat cooked in herbs; abgosht, meat cooked in thick milk with spices; rogan josh, richly spiced meat, cooked in curd, and coloured with the petals of the coxcomb flower; and gostaba and rishta—creamy kababs, and kormas, which are served at weddings and reflect the Mughal and Persian influence extending from Kashmir to Awadh and Hyderabad.

Awadh was part of the Kaushal kingdom, ruled by the Suryavanshi dynasty of Ayodhya. It reached the zenith of culinary art during the rein of the Nawabs of Awadh. Nawab Asaf-ud-Daulah was a great connoisseur of food and several bawarchikhanas or private kitchens flourished during his reign, resulting in a high degree of culinary skills. As many as a hundred dishes could be laid out on the dastarkhwan or ceremonial dinning table. Several culinary skills such as dumpukth cooking, and the preparation of kushtas were developed. Dumpukth cooking involves marinating the meat in curd, spices, herbs and dry fruit, sealing it in pots and cooking it over a low fire, thus preserving all the subtle flavours and aromas. Kushtas were pills made from the extracts of real rubies, pearls, gold, silver and saffron, etc. The pills were fed to the fowls for a few days, and used in incredible preparations of murgh korma, murgh musallam, murgh do piaza, kaju murgh, gulnar kababs, etc. It is said that a nawab who was a true connoisseur of food lost his teeth, but his appetite could still be satisfied with delicate melt-in-the-mouth kakori kababs. The murgh korma and kaju murgh with their white gravies of milk and almonds or curd and nuts were created to match the ambience of the Taj Mahal for Emperor Shah Jehan. Awadh cuisine is truly famous for its nazakat—delicacy, and nafasat—exquiteness.

For the last three hundred years, the history of Hyderabad has been marked by celebrations of the culinary art. The Nizam of Hyderabad, renowned for his miserliness, was very generous with his food. The royal gourmet cooks created great delicacies like shikampuri or stuffed kabab, nawabi murgh, korma or curries and the heavenly khurbani ka meetha made of puréed apricots.

In the east, Bengal abounds in rice, wheat, vegetables, geese, ducks, goats, sheep, pigs and fish of every variety. 'This is fertile kingdom!', exclaimed Bernier in AD 1660 as have many other European travellers. Bengal has been the home of sugarcane and fruits like lichi, pomelo and pineapple. Other crops include tea, coffee, maize, tapioca, cocoa, vanilla, ginger, cardamom, and mustard. Panchphoran—a mixture of five spices: onion seeds, celery seeds, aniseed, fenugreek and cumin lends aroma to delicious fish, meat and vegetables preparations. Cooking is considered an art here, and a Bengali meal runs from a bitter start to a sweet finish. A dish like shukto, made of neem leaves or bitter gourd is followed by rice with hot ghee, salt and green chillies. The next course consists of dal and a fish dish, accompanied by chutney and papad. The meal ends with a dessert of mishti, followed by a betel quid, which is a digestive. It is recorded that Swami Vivekananda enjoyed these preparations and the Bengali reformer Srinathacharya permitted Brahmins to eat meat, except on religious days.

In the north, shadowed by the virgin, snowy peaks of the Dhauladhar mountains, lie the lush green forests of the Kangra and Chamba valleys of Himachal Pradesh. Untouched by any invaders, it retains its Gujjar and Gaddi culture. The food here is reminiscent of the cuisine of the Indus Valley Civilization. Meats, grains, milk, ghee and rice are the mainstay of Pahadi, or hill cuisine. The royal cooks created exotic meat and chicken dishes like madra murgh, khatta gosht and chhaach gosht, using curd, milk, ghee and dry fruits as other ingredients. These dishes remain popular fare to this day.

In the west, the rolling sand dunes of Rajasthan, the desert ambience, the magnificent royal palaces and forts, the colourful festivals and dances, the bright hues of bandhini fabrics, the intricate silver jewellry and the spicy cuisine overpower the senses. The *Monasollasa* written by king Someshwara of Kalyana describes a whole pig being roasted on an open fire. Meat was marinated in spiced curd, placed with ghee in a wrapper and first baked then grilled on skewers. Meat preparations like sunthakhas—barbecued meat, chaklikhas—roasted seasoned pork, kavachandi—lamb fried with gram and spices, were the specialities served with batti, a hard roasted ball of wheat, which is cracked open and eaten with lashings of ghee. Khad murgh, lal murgh, sufaid murgh and makkai murgh are some of the dishes that have evolved over the years.

The sun-kissed beaches of Goa, with its resplendent coconut and palm trees—the land of feni, cashew nut and mango, was captured in AD 1510 from the Sultan of Bijapur by Alfonso d'Albuquerque, and the Estado da India, the Portuguese empire in India, was established. The Catholic monks of Goa developed a cuisine which amalgamated Iberian and Saraswat Hindu styles. Consequently, the different communities follow various cooking techniques today. For instance, the Goans from the north grind their masala and coconut separately, while those in the south prefer to grind them together, and then strain the gravy through a muslin cloth. While the Christians use vinegar, the Hindus prefer kokum, a sour Indian plum, to provide tang to their dishes. Though fish is popular with all Goans, the Hindus prefer lamb and chicken, and the Christians prefer pork. They use a periperi masala of mild red chillies and a cafreal masala of green chillies. A fiery button chilli is also used on occasion. Vinegar, tamarind, dried kokum, feni, spices, garlic and ginger are liberally used in dishes like sorpotel, pork assado, xacuti, prawn balchow and other fish preparations.

Further south, Andhra's fiery rich meat and seafood curries cooked in coconut milk are enhanced with flavours of gonkura—the sour leaf of *Hibiscus cannabinus*, tender green tamarind and raw mangoes in the traditional Telengana style of cooking.

In Mangalore, one finds unique innovations such as chicken stuffed dosas—a type of rice pancake, and chicken biryani made with spices and local herbs.

The Chettiar food of Tamil Nadu traces its origin to Andhra and is as fiery and rich. Meat, fish and other seafood dominate the cuisine, and are cooked in coconut milk, enhanced with the flavour of curry leaves.

The state of Kerala, long known as Chara, is historically a part of the Tamil cultural ambience. For centuries pepper, cardamoms, cloves, ginger, turmeric and other spices were shipped out from Kerala by the rulers and later by the Arabs, Portuguese, Dutch, and British. Its distinctive culinary feature was the use of black pepper. Meat was marinated in ground pepper and mustard seeds and then fried. It was also fried with pepper and tamarind. Kerala has been home to many religions. At least five religious groups live in harmony in the state and each community has its distinctive cuisine. The Muslims of

Kerala called Moplahs reflect the influence of the Arabs in their preparations of biryani and meat, and except for the Brahmin community, the others are non-vegetarian. Meat is generally cooked with spices and mellowed with coconut milk. It is served with curd, rice, rice roti, pachchadi, and pickle. The meal usually ends with a payasam. Famous meat specialties include erachi olathiyathu—meat and coconut fried without any extraneous fat, erachi thoran—steamed spiced meat and coconut and kappakari—fried meat and tapioca.

With the advent of colonial rule, some Western influences crept into Indian cuisine, as also the style of dining. While the cuisine continues to be diverse, and new features continue to be assimilated, Indian hospitality remains universally warm.

The concept of fine dining, the prominent role that good food enjoys in our way of life and our traditional hospitality, brings back early memories of banquets and garden parties held in my parents' home. English bone china, intricately folded serviettes, crystal glasses, silver cutlery and bowls of dry fruit, red roses in ornate vases on crisp white Irish linen graced elegantly decorated dining tables. Bearers dressed in spotless white uniforms and turbans serving the dishes on silver salvers heightened the romance and the glamour. A European meal started with salads arranged in small orange baskets, followed by soup, fish or chicken, and ended with desserts.

Indian food was individually served in large silver platters or thalis with eight to nine bowls or katoris of varying sizes, filled with rich kormas and saffron flavoured dry fruit gravies, accompanied by small silver platters of rice and biryani. Coffee, liqueurs and wafer thin dark chocolates with cigars were served after dinner in the drawing room. In the early days, men and women were served at separate tables laid out on different lawns or in different dining rooms. The men would be dressed in fine black tuxedoes and women in embroidered chiffon saris and brocade blouses with silk sleeves, usually white. Free intermingling of the sexes was uncommon.

Children were served early and put to bed. I remember once climbing up on to the terrace with my sisters and brothers, to peep into the drawing room and watch the banquet held to honour Sehgal, Dhillon and Shah Nawaz, the freedom fighters who had just been released from Red Fort, where they had been jailed. The drawing room, resounding to the sound of the National Anthem, is still etched in my memory.

Although the grandeur of the past is no longer a way of life in modern India, the splendour of its cuisine is still undiminished. I have had the opportunity to travel and taste, as well as share my experiences with my students. I have presented in this book a sampling of traditional recipes, culled over time, which I have improvised and innovated with chicken, to give you a flavour of Indian cuisine. Though these traditional dishes are delicious, most of them are high on fat. I offer my health conscious readers low fat alternatives to cook most of these delicacies, while still retaining the original flavours, aromas and taste.

Various reasons have led me to write a book on chicken dishes. Beef and pork are not acceptable as food items to some communities in India and the consumption of mutton has been scaled down by many because it is high in cholesterol. Chicken, on the other hand, is universally acceptable and medically recommended. It is low in cholesterol and high in protein, iron and vitamin B. It is easy to digest and succulent to eat.

Indian free-run chicken are less fatty than broiler chicken and have more flavour than the latter. However, consumption of broiler chicken is recommended, due to the hygienic conditions in which they are kept and also because cooking time is less.

In the following pages, I invite you to join me on a journey, as we explore the cooking traditions in this vast and colourful country. I hope you enjoy cooking and experimenting with these recipes, as much as I have enjoyed innovating and compiling them for you.

Bon Apetit.

SPICES

For centuries travellers and explorers risked life and limb to bring spices to Arabia and then to the Mediterranean and Europe. The Arabs held onto the trade for about a thousand years. The Romans then monopolized the trade to India for a while, before giving way to the Arabs again.

In the 1490s, the race began between the East and West to control the spice-land of India. The Portuguese explorers commandeered the spice trade from the Arabs. They brought the chilli from the New World. Pepper, cardamom, ginger, coriander and cumin were introduced to India's Malabar coast from the eastern Mediterranean via trade with the Arab world and Rome. On the east, the Coromandel coast had contacts with islands of Southeast Asia and China and imported nutmeg, mace and cloves.

In 1608, the first British ship arrived in Surat, near Bombay. By 1612 they had established maritime supremacy and forced Emperor Jehangir to give them trading concessions. The Portuguese, however, continued to control the pepper growing region, inland from the Malabar coast and only after harassing the Portuguese shipping, culminating in the treaty of Madrid in 1630, did the British get access to Goa, for loading spices.

Spices can be categorized as hot or fragrant. Some impart a distinct colour to a dish, along with their flavours.

Hot spices:
These spices stimulate the palate and sharpen the appetite as well as encourage the body to produce perspiration—a

good aid in keeping cool in a hot climate.

The best known of the hot spices include chillies and chilli powder (which is usually a blend of chillies and other spices); cayenne, ground from red chilli peppers, which is very strong and so should be sparingly used; and paprika, made from sweet peppers, which is fairly mild.

Peppercorn is a hot spice with a more aromatic flavour. Black, white, green and pink varieties are available. When sold together, they are known as tropical or mixed peppercorns.

Fragrant spices:
Spices such as allspice, cardamom, cloves, cinnamon, coriander, mace, juniper and nutmeg, add a pungent, sweet note to a variety of dishes—sweet and savoury. Most of these spices can be used whole or ground and they are usually added at the beginning of the cooking process, so that their flavour and aroma permeate and enhance the dish.

Colouring spices:
A dish can be coloured as well as flavoured by a spice. Saffron is the most expensive spice in the world, but only a pinch is needed to give a dish like paella a vibrant yellow colour. Turmeric imparts a rich yellow hue to many Indian dishes. It can be supplemented with saffron essence and used as a substitute for saffron.

The dark red colour of goulash and chouriço sausages comes from paprika.

Cooking with spices:
As spices need time to release their aroma and flavours, they are usually added near the start of the cooking process.

If the cooking process is prolonged, spices that are whole, cracked, or bruised are normally used rather than ground spices, which could become bitter. Large spices, such as cinnamon and cloves, are best removed before serving.

In oriental cooking, whole spices are roasted in a kadahi or heavy frying pan until they give out their aroma, before being ground. Roasting brings out the flavour of most spices, particularly if they are to be used in a dish that is cooked for a short time. Roast spices on low heat because they scorch easily. Use oil to prevent ground spices from scorching.

Spices should always be stored in airtight containers and kept in a cool dark, dry place.

Spices and their uses:

English Name	Hindi Name	Flavour and properties	Used In
All spice	Kabab cheeni	Sweet—a mixture of cloves and cinnamon	Meat curries, cakes, breads
Aniseed	Saunf	Sweet, aromatic; digestive	Kashmiri food, curries, meat, chicken, vegetables, pickles

English Name	Hindi Name	Flavour and properties	Used In
Asafoetida	Hing	Strong seasoning; Ant-acid	Curries, pickles, lentils
Bay leaves	Tej patta	Sweet	Curries, meat, rice
Black cardamom	Badi elaichi	Powerful, pungent	Garam masala, curries, biryani, savoury dishes
Black peppercorn	Kala mirch	Pungent; increases metabolic rate, improves blood circulation	Garam masala, meat, chicken, seafood, vegetarian dishes
Caraway seeds	Shahi jeera	Aromatic, strong	Mutton, chicken, rich gravy dishes
Carom seeds	Ajwain	Aromatic, strong; good digestive	Fish, gram flour batters, chickpeas, savoury dishes
Chilli powder	Lal mirch	Hot, very strong	Most Indian dishes
Cinnamon	Dal cheeni	Sweet, aromatic	Garam masala, curries, rice, sweet dishes, cakes, breads
Coriander seeds	Dhania	Fragrant, lemony	Curries, meat, chicken, vegetables, cakes, breads

English Name	Hindi Name	Flavour and properties	Used In
Cloves	Laung	Sweet, strong; healing properties	Garam masala, savoury and sweet dishes
Cumin seeds	Jeera	Pungent, slightly bitter, aromatic	Meat, seafood, vegetables, lentils, chutneys, pickles
Curry leaves	Curry patta	Aromatic	Curries
Dill	Sua	Tangy, pungent	Fish, beef, veal, potatoes, carrots, cucumber, eggs, cheese dishes
Fenugreek	Methi	Bitter, Strong; anti-diabetic	Garam masala, curries, pickles
Ginger (dry)	Sonth	Spicy, pungent; digestive	Kashmiri food, curries, fruit desserts, cakes, biscuits
Green cardamom	Chhoti elaichi	Sweet, pungent; digestive	Garam masala, curries, rice, sweet dishes
Mace	Javitri	Sweet, fragrant	Tandoori dishes, curries, cakes
Mustard	Rai	Pungent, hot	Curries, pickles, salad dressings

English Name	Hindi Name	Flavour and properties	Used In
Nutmeg	Jaiphal	Sweet, fragrant	Tandoori dishes, curries, cakes
Onion seeds	Kalaunji		Pickles, naan
Poppy seeds	Khus khus	Sweet, fragrant	Curries, desserts
Saffron	Kesar	Fragrant, yellow colour	Chicken, mutton, biryani, pulao, desserts
Sesame seeds	Til	Sweet, fragrant	Curries, desserts
Star anise	Badian or phool-chakra	Aromatic	Curries, biryani
Turmeric	Haldi	Distinct flavour; medicinal properties	Curries, vegetables, lentils, pulao

TABLE OF MEASURES

Metric Unit	Oz fl.oz	American Pint	American Cup	Imperial Pint	Imperial Cup
30	1				
60	2				
85	3				
115	4	¼	½		
140	5			¼	½
170	6				
200	7				
225	8	½	1	½	1
255	9				
285	10				
310	11				
340	12	¾			
370	13				
395	14				
430	15			¾	
455	16	1			
485	17				
510	18				
540	19				
570	20			1	
1 kg	2.2				
1 litre			2	1¾	

**The cup measure used in this book is an 8-oz cup
(225 ml)**

**1 tsp = 5 ml
1 tbsp = 3 tsp
A pinch = ⅛ tsp (literally a pinch)
All spoon measures are level**

EQUIVALENT QUANTITIES

Ground items:

Onion—fried and ground	1 cup =	265 gm
Cashew nut—ground	1 cup =	250 gm
Coconut—ground	1 cup =	260 gm
Ginger or garlic—ground	1¾ tsp =	10 gm

Dry fruits and nuts:

Almond—blanched and peeled	1 cup =	140 gm
Cashew nut—peeled	1 cup =	140 gm
Coconut—grated	1 cup =	80 gm
Coconut—desiccated	1 cup =	60 gm
Pistachio—blanched and peeled	1 cup =	140 gm
Groundnut—shelled and peeled	1 cup =	140 gm
Sultana (kishmish)	1 cup =	145 gm
Walnut—chopped	1 cup =	120 gm

Flour:

Wheat flour (atta)	1 cup =	120 gm
Refined flour (maida)	1 cup =	100 gm
All purpose flour	1 cup =	125 gm
Gram flour (besan)	1 cup =	80 gm

Cereals:

Rice	1 cup =	200 gm
Semolina	1 cup =	200 gm
Breadcrumbs	1 cup =	100 gm

Lentils:

Lentils (dal)	1 cup =	200 gm

Vegetables:

Coriander leaves—chopped	1 cup =	60 gm
	1 tbsp =	5 gm
Green peas—shelled	1 cup =	160 gm
Green peas—frozen	1 cup =	110 gm
Mint—chopped	1 cup =	60 gm
Potato—cubed	1 cup =	100 gm
Tomato—puréed	1 cup =	225 gm
Onion	1 large =	100 gm

Liquids:

Water	1 cup = 240 ml
Oil	1 cup = 220 ml

Fats:

Ghee (clarified butter)	1 cup =	225 gm
	1 tbsp =	15 gm
Vegetable ghee	1 cup =	200 gm

Dairy products:

Cream	1 cup =	240 ml
Milk	1 cup =	240 ml
Curd	1 cup =	225 gm
Hung curd	1 cup =	260 gm
Cheddar cheese—grated	1 cup =	110 gm
Khoya (dry condensed milk)	1 cup =	200 gm

Sugar:

Castor sugar	1 cup =	120 gm
Granulated sugar	1 cup =	200 gm

Spices:

Ajwain	2 tbsp = 15 gm
Aniseed (saunf)	2 tbsp = 15 gm
Black onion seeds (kalaunji)	1 tbsp = 10 gm
Black peppercorns	1 tbsp = 10 gm
Coriander seeds	1 tbsp = 5 gm
Cumin seeds	1 tbsp = 10 gm
Fenugreek seeds (methi dana)	1 tbsp = 15 gm
Dry fenugreek leaves (Kasuri methi)	1 tbsp = 15 gm
Melon seeds	1 tbsp = 10 gm
Pomegranate seeds (anar dana)	1 tbsp = 10 gm
Poppy seeds (khus khus)	1 tbsp = 10 gm
Sesame seeds (til)	1 tbsp = 10 gm
Sunflower seeds	1 tbsp = 10 gm
All powdered spices	1 tbsp = 10 gm

QUICK WAYS TO A HEALTHIER DIET

- Replace cream with low fat yoghurt or curd.
- Eat less red meat.
- Increase carbohydrates in meals and reduce proteins.
- Avoid canned food.
- Use whole wheat bread, flour and brown rice.
- Remove fat completely from meat and poultry.

- Drain fried food on paper towels.

- Leave on the nutritious skin of potatoes.

- Preferably grill, steam or stir-fry meat, seafood, poultry and vegetables.

- Avoid saturated fats—use sunflower or olive oil.

- Constant boiling or frying saturates oil. Avoid recycling oil.

- Reduce the total intake of fats and sugar. Replace with carbohydrates, fruits and vegetables.

HEALTHY COOKING TECHNIQUES

Steaming:
Arrange vegetables in a metal steamer and place over a saucepan of boiling water, or steam in a pressure cooker to retain their nutrients.

Grilling and barbecuing:
Lightly brush vegetables with oil and grill or barbecue, to prevent them from drying. Meat already has fat on it, which melts and drips away making grilled and barbecued meat fat-free.

Stir-frying:
Meat and vegetables can be stir-fried in a very small quantity of oil, in a non-stick pan, thus retaining their

nutrients, texture and flavour.

Microwave Cooking:
Microwave ovens speed up the cooking process thus retaining the essential nutrients in the food. Many types of meat and seafood can be cooked without fats in a microwave oven.

BASIC RECIPES AND COOKING TECHNIQUES FOR INDIAN CUISINE

DAHI

Curd

1 litre milk
1 tbsp curd

- Bring milk to boil and cool till lukewarm.
- Mix one tablespoon curd with a little milk and mix into remaining milk. Whisk well.
- Pour milk into a bowl. Cover bowl and leave to set in a warm place for 7-8 hours.
- Do not shake the bowl while curd is setting, else it will not set properly.

Note: The temperature of the milk is important. If it is too hot, the dahi will become sour and if it is cold, it will not set properly.

If curd is not available, use one tablespoon lime juice.

HUNG CURD

Place curd in a muslin bag and hang for 3-4 hours. Place a bowl below the bag to catch the drippings.

- The curd in the bag is called hung curd.
- Cream cheese may be used as a substitute.

PANEER

Cottage Cheese

1 litre full cream milk
1 cup curd, beaten till smooth
1 tsp lime juice

- Place milk in a pan and bring to boil.
- Add in beaten curd and lime juice.
- Keep milk boiling and stir continuously till it curdles and the whey separates.
- Strain through a muslin cloth.
- Tie muslin cloth and hang for one hour with a bowl beneath it to catch the drippings.
- Place muslin bag on a plate. Place a chopping board over it, with a weight on top. Allow the remaining whey to ooze out for another one hour.
- Remove paneer from cloth and keep in a refrigerator.
- Paneer can be refrigerated for 2 days or frozen in a deep freezer, where it will stay indefinitely.

KHOYA

Dry Condensed Milk

1 litre milk

- Bring milk to boil in a non-stick kadahi or wok.

- Lower heat and cook stirring continuously till it forms a thick ball.

- Remove from heat.

- Cool and store in a refrigerator or deep freezer.

COCONUT MILK

1 medium-sized coconut
2 cups hot water

- Grate white part of coconut.

- Soak grated coconut in hot water for 10 minutes.

- Blend in a liquidizer or food processor.

- Strain liquid through a muslin cloth. Squeeze cloth to extract all liquid. This is the thick coconut milk.

- Blend strained coconut with 2 cups water again and extract the liquid. This is the thin coconut milk.

Note: Thick coconut milk is usually added towards the end of the cooking process, while the thin milk may be added earlier.

TAMARIND WATER

1 tbsp tamarind, seeds and strings removed
2 tbsp hot water

- Wash tamarind and add to hot water. Allow to soak for 15-20 minutes.

- Squeeze with your hand and strain the juice, which is called tamarind water or juice.

FRESH TOMATO PURÉE

- Boil whole tomatoes in water for 5 minutes. Drain out water.

- Remove skin and purée tomatoes in a liquidizer or food processor.

- Strain and use.

- One cup of tomato purée is made from 3 large tomatoes.

CHICKEN STOCK

Chicken bones can be utilized to make a very rich, tasty and nourishing stock. It can be used in place of water, for soups or gravies and for cooking rice.

- Cook ½ kg chicken bones with ½ tsp garlic, ginger and salt in 6 cups of water, in a pressure cooker for 25 minutes.

- Strain stock and use as required.

ONIONS, GINGER AND GARLIC

Onions may be cut into small pieces and processed in a liquidizer or food processor without water, to save time and 'onion tears', to produce a ground paste. If they are chopped or sliced by hand, they should be finely and evenly chopped or sliced.

Ginger and garlic may be ground in an electric grinder and stored in a glass jar in a refrigerator for 4-5 days.

Onions, ginger and garlic should be fried in a non-stick pan, on moderately low heat in oil, as stipulated by the recipe. If the paste sticks to the pan, add a little water and continue frying to get the required colour. This paste can be made in advance and kept in the refrigerator for 4-5 days. It can also be frozen and used as required.

DRY ROASTING OF SPICES

Spices should be dry roasted before grinding. This enhances the aroma and flavour of the spices.

Heat a tava, griddle or non-stick pan and lightly roast, individually, whole spices like cinnamon, cardamom, cloves, peppercorns, coriander seeds, cumin seeds, etc, over moderate heat for 5-6 minutes.

Cool and grind to a powder in an electric grinder.

BLENDING AND GRINDING OF INGREDIENTS

The term *grinding* in this book is used for powdering of dry ingredients. It is also used when ingredients like ginger, garlic, etc are to be made into a paste.

Blending on the other hand, is a mixing action to ensure that the ingredients attain a smooth and uniform texture.

DUMPUKHT COOKING

The term denotes the baking of meat within a seal of dough. It is a Persian word meaning air-cooked or baked. The word was anglicized to dumpoke in Colonial India and frequently denoted a boneless fowl, stuffed with spices, almonds and raisins, stewed in butter and cooked in a pan sealed with dough. The Kannada writer Shantinatha referred to slow cooking under a seal of wheat dough to hold down the lid as early as AD 1068. This style of cooking results in the retention and permeation of the flavors of the ingredients.

Make a paste of flour and water. Cover pan with a lid and seal lid onto pan with the paste. Place pan on a tava or griddle and cook on minimum heat.

A moderately hot oven at 150°C-180°C (300°F-350°F) is a very convenient alternative. Pressure cooking over minimum heat is also a good alternative.

TANDOORI COOKING

Tandoori cooking consists of marinating fish, mutton or chicken in curd mixed with spices and herbs for long hours and then baking in a clay oven called a tandoor. Baking in a tandoor oven implies cooking with dry heat, similar to roasting or barbecuing. Since it is not possible to have clay ovens in modern homes, an electric or gas oven may be used as an alternative and I have used them quite successfully.

Grilling is done at a high temperature, so that the flavours and juices are sealed in and the nutritive value of the food is retained.

Tandoori food is fat free and offers a simple, easy method of cooking. Served with fresh salads, it makes a delicious meal.

Usual accompaniments to tandoori food are mint chutney mixed with curd, pickled onion or onion relish and roomali roti, tandoori roti or naan.

Chicken tikka rolled in roomali roti makes an exotic snack.

BALTI COOKING

The traditional Indian kadahi cooking has been influenced by far eastern wok cooking, so that shredded or diced meat is stir fried in a minimum of fat. Cooking time is minimized and the flavour and nutritive value of the food is retained.

This form of cooking has been termed balti cooking in Europe and has gained great popularity there, because of the European emphasis on low fat food.

Dishes cooked in this manner can be served with chutney, pickled onions or onion relish and naan, roti, roomali roti, layered parantha, plain boiled rice or even pasta.

DRY MASALAS

Garam Masala

50 gm (8½ tbsp) coriander seeds
25 gm (3 tbsp) cumin seeds
12 gm (1⅓ tbsp) cloves
12 gm (24 pieces, 1" each) cinnamon
12 gm (15) whole black cardamoms
12 gm (1⅓ tbsp) black peppercorn

- Grind all ingredients and store in an airtight jar.

Kashmiri Garam Masala

50 gm cumin seeds
50 gm cinnamon
50 gm whole black cardamoms
10 gm whole green cardamoms
20 gm cloves
20 gm black peppercorn
10 gm caraway seeds (shahi jeera)
5-6 flowers mace (javitri)
15 bay leaves (tej patta)
10 gm (3" piece) dry ginger
1 nutmeg

- Toast each ingredient except nutmeg separately on a

tava or griddle. Cool and grind all ingredients. Store in an airtight jar.

Konkani Masala

125 gm coriander seeds
2 tbsp Bengal gram (chané ki dal)
2 tbsp rice
1 tbsp cumin seeds
2 tsp aniseed (saunf)
1 tsp turmeric powder
250 gm chilli powder

- Roast each ingredient, except chilli powder, individually on a tava or griddle. Cool and grind. Mix in chilli powder. Store in an airtight jar.

Chaat Masala

1 tsp cumin seeds
1 tsp dry pomegranate seeds (anar dana)
1 tsp black salt (kala namak)
2 tsp dry mango powder (amchur)
½ tsp salt
½ tsp chilli powder
½ tsp powdered dry ginger (sonth)
½ tsp powdered black pepper
A pinch of asafoetida

- Roast cumin seeds on a tava or griddle till light brown. Cool and grind to a powder. Grind pomegranate seeds to a powder. Mix all ingredients. Store in an airtight jar.

Salads

MURGH PHALHAR SALAD

Chicken Salad with Honey and Mint Dressing

Serves: 4

½ kg chicken, boiled and shredded
1 cup diced pineapple
2 spring onions, sliced
1 red capsicum, sliced

Dressing:

2 tbsp olive oil
4 tbsp orange juice
1 tsp honey
2 mint leaves, chopped
½ tsp salt
¼ tsp mustard powder
¼ tsp powdered black pepper
½ cup thick cream

Garnish:

4-5 olives
2 oranges

- Peel oranges and remove pith and seeds from segments.

- Blend ingredients for dressing in a liquidizer or food processor. Add remaining ingredients except garnish. Mix well and arrange salad on a flat dish.

- Garnish with olives and orange slices.

MURGH DILPASAND SALAD

Chicken Salad with Cream Cheese Dressing

Serves: 4

1 kg chicken, whole or jointed
1 tsp ground garlic
1 tsp ground ginger
1 onion, chopped
1 tsp salt
½ cup cream

Dressing:

1 cup hung curd or cream cheese
1 tsp salt
1 tsp powdered black pepper
½ tsp mustard powder
2 green chillies, chopped
2 tbsp chopped coriander leaves
2 tbsp chopped spring onions
1 tbsp lime juice

Garnish:

1 cup chopped lettuce
3 slices pineapple
1 capsicum, shredded
1 cup chopped walnuts

- Cook chicken with garlic, ginger, onion, salt and 2 cups water over low heat for 25-30 minutes, till tender.

- Cool and shred chicken meat.

- Blend ingredients for dressing in a liquidizer or food processor and mix in cream. Add to chicken and mix well.

- Spread chicken salad on a flat serving dish. Arrange lettuce and pineapple slices around chicken.

- Garnish top with capsicum and walnuts.

CHATPATA MURGH SALAD

Tangy Chicken Salad

Serves: 4

1 kg chicken, whole or jointed
1 tsp ground garlic
1 tsp ground ginger
1 onion, chopped
1 tsp salt

Dressing:

4 tbsp lime juice
2 tbsp chopped green chillies
2 tbsp chopped coriander leaves
2 tbsp chopped mint leaves
1 onion, chopped
1 tsp salt
½ tsp chilli powder
½ tsp powdered roasted caraway seeds (shahi jeera)
½ tsp dry mango powder (amchur)
¼ tsp powdered black salt (kala namak)

Garnish:

2 potatoes, diced and fried

- Cook chicken with garlic, ginger, onion, salt and 2 cups water over low heat for 25 minutes, till tender. Cool and shred chicken meat.

- Mix ingredients for dressing. Add chicken.

- Arrange salad on a platter and garnish with fried diced potatoes.

MURGH AUR RAJMAH SALAD

Chicken and Kidney Bean Salad

Serves: 4

200 gm chicken sausages, sliced
100 gm (1 cup) kidney beans (rajmah)
2 tbsp salad oil

Dressing:

2 tbsp vinegar
3 tbsp red wine
2 spring onions, chopped
1 tsp salt
½ tbsp powdered coriander seeds
½ tbsp powdered cloves
½ tbsp powdered black peppercorn

Garnish:

100 gm lettuce, shredded
1 white radish, shredded

- Soak beans in 2 cups water for 7-8 hours. Cook in a pressure cooker for 25 minutes. Drain beans.
- Mix all ingredients for dressing in a pan. Bring to boil. Remove pan from heat immediately.
- Mix together sausages, beans, dressing and oil. Allow to marinate for one hour.
- Place salad on a platter and garnish with radish and lettuce.

MURGH AUR MAKKAI SALAD

Chicken and Corn Salad with Vinaigrette Dressing

Serves: 4

¼ kg boneless chicken, boiled and shredded
100 gm (1 cup) boiled corn off the cob or baby corn
2 green capsicum, sliced

Dressing:

2 tbsp salad oil or olive oil
1 tbsp vinegar
1 tbsp lime juice
½ tsp salt
½ tsp chilli powder
½ tsp sugar
½ tsp mustard powder
5-6 basil or tulsi leaves, chopped
6-7 mint leaves, chopped
1 bay leaf (tej patta), powdered

Garnish:

1 cup bean sprouts
2 tomatoes, quartered

- Blend ingredients for dressing in a liquidizer or food processor.

- Mix chicken, corn, capsicum and dressing and chill.

- Place salad on a platter and serve garnished with quartered tomatoes and bean sprouts.

Snacks

HARYALI MURGH TIKKA

Barbecued Chicken in Green Herbs

Serves: 4

½ kg boneless chicken, cut into 3" cubes

Marinade:

½ cup curd, beaten till smooth
1 tsp ground ginger
1 tsp ground garlic
4 tbsp chopped coriander leaves
1 tbsp chopped capsicum
1 tbsp chopped spinach
1 tbsp chopped mint leaves
1 tbsp chopped green chillies
1 tbsp lime juice
1 tsp salt
1½ tsp dry fenugreek leaves (kasuri methi), crumbled
½ tsp red chilli powder
½ tsp garam masala powder

Garnish:

Onion rings
Lime slices

- Blend all ingredients for marinade, except powdered spices in a liquidizer or food processor to a smooth paste. Mix in powdered spices. Add chicken pieces and allow to marinate for 3-4 hours.

- Grill chicken at 220°C (425°F) for 3-4 minutes on each side, or barbecue on a charcoal fire for 4-5 minutes. If your grill is not graded in degrees, then grill at maximum temperature.

- Arrange chicken in a dish and garnish with onion rings and lime slices.

- Serve with naan or roomali roti.

MURGH MALAI TIKKA

Grilled Creamy Chicken

Serves: 4

You will need skewers to prepare this dish.

½ kg boneless chicken, cut into 1½" cubes
Butter for basting

First marinade:

½ cup thick curd, beaten till smooth
1 tsp ground garlic
1 tsp ground ginger
1 tsp salt
½ tsp pepper
1 tbsp lime juice

Second marinade:

½ cup grated cheddar cheese
3 tbsp ground cashew nuts
1 egg, lightly beaten
1 tsp ground coriander leaves
1 tsp ground green chillies
¼ tsp powdered mace
¼ tsp powdered nutmeg
2 tbsp cornflour
½ cup thick cream

- Mix all ingredients for first marinade to a smooth paste and marinate chicken for one hour.

- Mix all ingredients for second marinade, add to

Snacks　　　　**13**

chicken and mix well.

- Keep in a refrigerator for 2 hours.

- Bring chicken to room temperature and pierce chicken pieces onto skewers.

- Grill in a regular clay or gas tandoor or barbecue on a charcoal fire for 6-7 minutes, basting with butter, till golden brown. You may also grill in an electric grill for 5 minutes.

- Remove chicken from skewers, place in a dish and serve with naan or roomali roti.

ACHARI MURGH TIKKA

Barbecued Pickled Chicken

Serves: 4

½ kg boneless chicken, cut into 3" cubes

Marinade:

½ cup curd, beaten till smooth
1 tsp ground garlic
1 tsp ground ginger
½ tsp powdered black pepper
½ tsp chilli powder
1 tsp salt
1 tbsp lime juice
½ tsp powdered aniseed (saunf)
½ tsp powdered onion seeds (kalaunji)
½ tsp powdered fenugreek seeds
1 tbsp mustard oil

Garnish:

Onion slices

- Mix all ingredients for marinade to a smooth paste. Add chicken, mix well and allow to marinate for 3-4 hours.

- Grill chicken at 220°C (425°F) for 4-5 minutes. If your grill is not graded in degrees, then grill at maximum temperature.

- You can also put chicken pieces on skewers and barbecue over a charcoal fire for 4-5 minutes, or roast in an oven at 220°C (425°F) for 4-5 minutes.

- Arrange chicken in a dish, garnish with onion slices and serve with naan or roomali roti.

TANDOORI MURGH

Tandoori Chicken

Serves: 2

1 kg chicken without skin, kept whole, cut into 4 or jointed as
desired
Butter or ghee for basting

Marinade:

½ cup thick curd, beaten till smooth
1 tsp ground garlic
1 tsp ground ginger
1 tsp ground coriander leaves
1 tsp ground green chillies
½ tsp ground mint leaves
1 tsp salt
1 tsp garam masala powder
1½ tsp chilli powder
¼ tsp powdered mace (javitri)
¼ tsp tenderon powder or 1 tbsp raw papaya
3 tsp raw papaya juice
1 tbsp lime juice or vinegar
½ tsp red food colouring powder

Garnish:

Chaat masala
Onion rings
Lime slices

- Make deep gashes in chicken flesh.
- Squeeze off excess water from chicken and leave to
  dry for 15 minutes.

- Mix all ingredients for marinade to a smooth paste.

- Add chicken pieces, mix well and allow to marinate for 6 hours outside the refrigerator. If the weather is very hot, reduce marinating time at room temperature to 4 hours.

- Grill in a regular clay or gas tandoor, or on a charcoal fire, till chicken is deep red and black streaks begin to appear. It should take about 20-25 minutes.

- The chicken can be grilled in an electric gill at 220°C (425°F) for 7-8 minutes on each side or roasted in an oven at 220°C (425°F) for 12-15 minutes. If your grill is not graded in degrees, then grill at maximum temperature.

- Baste chicken pieces with butter or ghee while cooking.

- Arrange chicken on a platter, sprinkle with chaat masala and garnish with onion rings and lime slices.

- Serve with naan or roomali roti.

TANDOORI·KALMI

Tandoori Chicken Drumsticks

Serves: 4

½ kg chicken drumsticks

Marinade:

3-4 whole green cardamoms
3 cloves
2 pieces cinnamon, 1" each
1 tsp poppy seeds (khus khus)
2 star anise (badian)
1 tsp chilli powder
1 tsp coriander seeds
½ tsp turmeric powder
1 tsp ground garlic
1 tsp ground ginger
1 tsp salt
½ cup thick curd, beaten till smooth

Garnish:

Shredded onion

- Grind all ingredients for marinade except curd.

- Mix ground spices with curd. Apply to chicken and allow to marinate for 2-4 hours.

- Grill in a regular clay or gas tandoor, or barbecue over a coal fire for 9-10 minutes. It can also be baked in an oven at 220°C (425°F) for 9-10 minutes, or shallow fried.

- Arrange chicken drumsticks on a platter and garnish with shredded onions.

- Serve with mint chutney, onion relish and naan.

KALMI KABAB

Barbecued Chicken Drumsticks

Serves: 4

½ kg chicken drumsticks
Butter as required

Marinade:

½ cup thick curd, beaten till smooth
1 tsp ground garlic
1 tsp ground ginger
1 tsp ground green chillies
1 tsp ground coriander leaves
1 tsp ground raw papaya
1 tsp salt
1 tsp chilli powder
1 tsp garam masala powder
1 tbsp lime juice

Garnish:

Onion rings

- Make deep cuts in chicken flesh.
- Mix all ingredients for marinade to a smooth paste.
- Add chicken and marinate for 6 hours.
- Grill chicken in a regular clay or gas tandoor, or barbecue on a charcoal fire for about 15-20 minutes, till tender. It can also be baked in an oven at 220°C (425°F) for 9-10 minutes.

- Brush chicken with butter and cover bone with foil for easy handling, while eating.

- Arrange chicken on a platter and garnish with onion rings.

- Serve with 2 tablespoons mint chutney mixed with half cup curd.

KALMI BEGUM BAHAR

Grilled Chicken Drumsticks in Green Herbs

Serves: 4

1 kg chicken drumsticks
Butter for basting

Marinade:

½ cup thick curd, beaten till smooth
1 tsp ground garlic
1 tsp ground ginger
1 tbsp grated onion
1 tbsp ground capsicum
1 tbsp ground coriander leaves
1 tsp ground mint leaves
1 tsp ground green chillies
1 tsp salt
1 tsp garam masala powder
1 tbsp lime juice

Garnish:

1 tsp powdered caraway seeds (shahi jeera)

- Wash chicken drumsticks and dry. Make deep cuts in the flesh.

- Mix all ingredients for marinade to a smooth paste. Add to chicken and allow to marinate for 6 hours.

- Grill in a tandoor or barbecue on a charcoal fire for 8-9 minutes on either side, till done and light brown. Baste with butter while grilling.

- Arrange chicken on a platter, sprinkle with caraway seed powder and serve with naan or tandoori roti and sliced onions soaked in vinegar.

TANDOORI MURGH PAKORA

Tandoori Chicken Fritters

Serves: 4

This recipe is an innovated one—chicken is marinated in curd mixed with tandoori masala but fried instead of being baked in a tandoor.

½ kg boneless chicken breast, cut into 3" cubes
Oil for deep frying

Marinade:

½ cup curd, beaten till smooth
1 tsp ground garlic
1 tsp ground ginger
1 tbsp lime juice
1 tsp ground mint leaves

Batter:

100 gm (1¼ cups) gram flour (besan)
1½ tsp salt
1½ tsp chilli powder
1 tsp dry mango powder (amchur)
1 tsp ajwain
½ tsp garam masala powder
½ tsp tandoori red colour
¼ tsp asafoetida (hing)
¾ cup water

Garnish:

Chaat masala

- Mix all ingredients for marinade.

- Add chicken to marinade, mix well and allow to marinate for 2 hours.

- Mix all ingredients for batter in a bowl and beat well. The batter should have a thick flowing consistency.

- Add marinated chicken to batter and leave for half an hour.

- Deep fry chicken in hot oil till crisp.

- Place pakoras on a platter, sprinkle with chaat masala and serve with mint chutney, onion relish and naan.

Note: Please be sure to use food colour from a recognized and reputed brand.

MURGH KI CHHARRIA

Chicken Lollipops

Serves: 5-6

Chicken lollipops are chicken wings cut into two at the joint. The meat is scraped off the bone and moved to one end. These are readily available in most meat shops.

½ kg chicken lollipops
Oil for deep frying

Batter:

150 gm (1½ cups) flour (maida)
1 tsp ground garlic
1 tsp ground ginger
1 tsp salt
1 tsp chilli powder
¼ tsp baking powder
½ tsp ground pomegranate seeds (anar dana)
½ tsp garam masala powder
¾ cup water

- Mix all dry ingredients for batter. Gradually beat in water to make a batter of thick flowing consistency.

- Marinate chicken in batter for 2-3 hours.

- Deep fry chicken in oil, over medium heat, till crisp. Drain well.

- Cover bone with foil for easy handling, while eating.

- Arrange chicken on a platter and serve with mint chutney.

MURGH SEEKH KABAB

Barbecued Chicken Kabab

Serves: 6

You will need skewers to prepare this dish.

½ kg chicken mince
1 tsp salt
½ tsp powdered mace (javitri)
1 tsp garam masala powder
¼ tsp powdered nutmeg
3 tsp cornflour
2 tsp powdered poppy seeds (khus khus)
3 tsp ground almonds
1 tsp ground garlic
1 tsp ground ginger
1 tbsp chopped coriander leaves
1 tbsp chopped green chillies
1 egg, lightly beaten
Oil or butter for basting

Garnish:

Onion or limes slices

- Do not wash mince.
- Mix all ingredients except egg and oil or butter and grind to a smooth paste.
- Add egg and mix well.
- Keep mixture in a refrigerator for at least one hour to achieve a better texture.

- Divide mixture into 18 portions.

- Grease your hands and skewers with oil. Shape one portion of mince into a sausage and thread onto a skewer. Press into a thin seekh kabab, 4 inches long. Make all kababs in the same way.

- Grill kababs over a charcoal fire for 2 minutes, rotating skewers. Brush kababs with oil or butter and grill for a further minute till golden brown.

- Remove kababs from skewers, arrange on a platter and garnish with onion or lime slices.

- Serve with naan or roomali roti and mint or coriander and coconut chutney.

Note: The kababs may be grilled in a regular clay or gas tandoor at moderate heat, or in an electric grill.

AFGHANI GEELAFI SEEKH KABAB

Barbecued Chicken Kabab – Afghan Style

Serves: 6

You will need skewers to prepare this dish.

500 gm chicken mince
¼ cup grated cottage cheese (paneer)
2 tbsp ground almonds
1 tsp garam masala powder
1 tsp chilli powder
1 tsp salt
1 tsp ground garlic
1 tsp ground ginger
1 tsp ground coriander leaves
1 tsp ground green chillies
1 tsp powdered dry fenugreek leaves (kasuri methi)
1 tbsp lime juice
2 tbsp grated onion
1 egg, lightly beaten
2 tbsp oil
Butter for basting

Garnish:

Onion rings
Lime slices

- Mix all ingredients except egg, oil and butter. Knead well to make a smooth paste.

- Mix in egg.

- Chill in a refrigerator for one hour.

- Divide mince into 16 portions.

- Grease your hands and skewers with oil. Shape one portion of mince into a sausage and thread onto a skewer. Press into a thin seekh kabab, 4 inches long. Make all kababs in the same way.

- Grill or barbecue kababs for 2-3 minutes, rotating skewers and basting with butter.

- Remove kababs from skewers, arrange on a platter and garnish with lime slices and onion rings.

- Serve with naan or roomali roti.

Note: The stuffing used for murgh shammi kabab can also be filled into these.

HARÉ BHARÉ MURGH KABAB

Stuffed Chicken Kabab

Serves: 4

Mince:

200 gm chicken mince
1 cup washed and chopped spinach
2 slices fresh bread, crusts removed if desired
1 tbsp freshly ground spinach
1 tsp salt
1 tsp chilli powder
1 tsp garam masala powder

Filling:

100 gm mashed cottage cheese (paneer)
2 tbsp mint or coriander chutney

Semolina as required
Oil for shallow frying

- Mix all ingredients for filling.
- Mix all ingredients for mince into a smooth paste.
- Divide into 12 portions.
- Flatten each portion of mince into a disc. Put one teaspoon filling on disc. Work mince around to cover filling and gently shape into a flat round kabab.
- Roll each kabab in semolina.

- Shallow fry in oil, in a non-stick pan, till cooked through and brown.

- Arrange kababs in a dish and serve with mint chutney, onion relish and naan.

Note: To make a kofta curry, shape into balls, deep fry in oil till crisp and add to a tomato gravy (see recipe Nargisi kofta curry) and serve with roti or naan.

SHIKAMPURI MURGH KABAB

Stuffed Chicken Kabab

Serves: 4

Mince:

¾ kg chicken mince
1 large onion, grated
2 tbsp Bengal gram (chané ki dal)
1 tsp ground garlic
½ tsp salt
½ tsp chilli powder
1 tsp garam masala powder
1 egg, lightly beaten

Filling:

200 gm hung curd or cream cheese
2 tbsp ground mint leaves
1 tsp salt
1 tsp pepper

Garnish:

Onion rings
Lime slices

Oil for shallow frying

- Place all ingredients for mince, except egg, in a pressure cooker with three-quarter cup water.
- Cook under pressure for 10 minutes.
- Allow cooker to cool before opening.

- Open cooker and cook mince on low heat to dry out any liquid.

- Grind to a smooth paste.

- Add egg and mix well.

- Mix all ingredients for filling to a smooth paste.

- Divide mince mixture into 16 portions.

- Flatten one portion and place one teaspoon filling in the centre. Work mince around to cover filling and gently shape into a flat round kabab. Make remaining kababs in the same way.

- Shallow fry kababs in oil till light brown.

- Place on kitchen towel to drain off excess oil.

- Arrange kababs on a platter, garnish with onion rings and lime slices and serve with naan or roomali roti.

MURGH SHAMMI KABAB

Chicken Kabab Stuffed with Dry Fruit

Serves: 6

½ kg chicken mince
1 large onion, grated or ground
1 tsp ground garlic
1 tsp salt
½ tsp chilli powder
¼ tsp turmeric powder
2 tbsp Bengal gram (chané ki dal)
½ cup water
1 tbsp chopped coriander leaves
1 tbsp chopped green chillies
1 tbsp chopped ginger
1 tsp garam masala powder
1 egg, lightly beaten
Oil for shallow frying

Stuffing:

1 tbsp oil
1 small onion, chopped
2-3 green chillies, chopped
1 tbsp chopped almonds or cashew nuts
1 tbsp chopped sultanas (kishmish)
¼ tsp salt
¼ tsp chilli powder
¼ tsp garam masala powder

Garnish:

Onion rings
Lime slices

- Put mince and next 7 ingredients in a pressure cooker and cook for 20 minutes under pressure.

- Remove cooker from heat and allow mince to cool.

- Add next 4 ingredients to mince and grind to a smooth paste.

- Add egg and mix well.

- Heat oil for stuffing in a non-stick pan.

- Lightly fry onion.

- Add chillies, nuts and sultanas. Fry for a few seconds.

- Stir in salt and powdered spices and remove from heat.

- Divide mince paste into 16 portions.

- Flatten one portion of mince into a round disc. Place one teaspoon filling in the centre and work mince around to cover filling. Gently shape into a flat round kabab. Make remaining kababs in the same way.

- Shallow fry kababs in oil, in a non-stick pan till brown on both sides. Place kababs on paper towels to drain excess oil.

- Arrange kababs on a platter, garnish with onion rings and lime slices and serve with mint or coriander and coconut chutney.

MURGH KATHI KABAB

Chicken Rolls

Serves: 4

Chicken:

½ kg boneless chicken, cut into 1" cubes
2 tbsp oil
1 tbsp chopped coriander leaves
1 tbsp chopped green chillies
1 onion, sliced
1 tbsp lime juice

Marinade:

1 tsp ground ginger
1 tsp ground garlic
1 tsp chilli powder
1 tsp garam masala powder
1 tsp salt
1 tsp ground mint leaves
½ cup curd, beaten till smooth

Roti:

200 gm flour (maida)
50 gm whole wheat flour (atta)
½ cup milk
1 tbsp oil

- Mix ingredients for marinade and add chicken. Allow to marinate for 2 hours.

- Heat oil for chicken in a non-stick pan and add chicken. Cook till oil starts to bubble on top.

- Add remaining ingredients, stir and remove from heat.

- Mix all ingredients for roti with a little water and knead into a soft dough. Cover and allow to rest for one hour.

- Pinch off a lime-sized piece of dough and roll into a round 5 inches in diameter.

- Roast on a tava or griddle on both sides for 1-2 minutes, making sure the roti remains soft.

- Make remaining roti in the same way.

- Spread 3 tablespoons of filling on one side of each roti and roll. Wrap in foil to keep warm.

Note: ½ teaspoon dry mango powder (amchur) may be added to the marinade for extra flavour.

MURGH KANDAHARI

Grilled Chicken – Kandahar Style

Serves: 4

500 gm chicken breasts
2 tbsp pomegranate juice
1 tsp chilli powder
½ cup thick curd, beaten till smooth
1 tsp ground garlic
1 tsp ground ginger
1 tsp garam masala powder
1 tsp caraway seeds (shahi jeera)
1 tsp salt
½ tsp powdered black pepper
A few strands of saffron
2 tsp butter for basting

Garnish:

Onion rings
Lime slices

- Wash chicken and dry. Make deep cuts in chicken flesh.

- Mix pomegranate juice and chilli powder. Rub into chicken and allow to marinate for half an hour.

- Mix remaining ingredients, except butter. Rub into chicken and marinate for a further 3-4 hours.

- Grill chicken in a regular clay or gas tandoor, or electric grill, or barbecue over a charcoal fire for 6-7 minutes on each side. You may bake the chicken in an oven at 220°C (425°F).

- Baste with butter while grilling.
- Place chicken in a dish and garnish with onion rings and lime slices and serve.

KOZHI DOSA

Stuffed Pancakes

Serves: 4

Batter:

1 cup husked black beans (urad ki dal)
1½ cups boiled rice
1½ cups broken basmati rice
¼ cup Bengal gram (chané ki dal)
1 tsp salt
1 tsp chilli powder
¼ tsp asafoetida powder (hing)
1 tsp ground garlic

Filling:

½ kg boneless chicken, shredded
2 tbsp mustard oil
½ tsp ground ginger
½ tsp ground garlic
½ tsp mustard seeds, coarsely ground
½ tsp aniseed (saunf), coarsely ground
¼ tsp asafoetida powder (hing)
1 tsp chilli powder
1 tsp garam masala
1 tsp salt
½ tsp turmeric powder

Coconut oil for frying

- To prepare batter wash both dals and broken rice, and soak with boiled rice in plenty of water for 8-10 hours.

- Drain water and grind dal and rice in a liquidizer or food processor to a slightly grainy texture.

- Add remaining ingredients and enough water to achieve a thick flowing consistency.

- Whip mixture with hand till fluffy.

- Keep aside for 8 hours to ferment.

- Heat mustard oil for filling in a non-stick pan till smoking. Lower heat and add ginger and garlic. Fry for one minute.

- Add mustard seeds, aniseed and asafoetida and fry for one minute.

- Add chicken with remaining ingredients and continue to fry for a further 5-6 minutes.

- Heat one teaspoon coconut oil in a non-stick frying pan, tava or dosa pan.

- Pour in one ladle of batter and spread with a circular motion of the ladle to make a pancake as thin as possible. Fry till base is golden and top is soft and fluffy.

- Place 4 tablespoons of filling in the centre of the dosa, fold over and serve immediately.

Main Course Dishes

BALTI ACHARI MURGH

Pickled Shredded Chicken

Serves: 4

½ kg boneless chicken, shredded
2 tbsp mustard oil
2 dry red chillies
1 tsp ground garlic
1 tsp ground ginger
¼ tsp asafoetida (hing)
1 tsp chilli powder
1 tsp garam masala powder
½ tsp turmeric powder
1 tsp salt
1 cup chicken stock or water

Grind Coarsely:

1 tsp onion seeds (kalaunji)
1 tsp fenugreek seeds (methi)
1 tsp mustard seeds
1 tsp aniseed (saunf)

- Heat oil to smoking point in a non-stick kadahi or wok.

- Add dry red chillies, reduce heat and add garlic and ginger. Stir and fry for one minute.

- Add coarsely ground spices and asafoetida. Stir and fry for a further minute.

- Stir in chicken, powdered spices and salt and fry for 5-6 minutes, stirring continuously.

- Add one cup stock or water and simmer on low heat for 6-7 minutes.

- Serve with plain boiled rice, tandoori roti, roomali roti or naan and a salad of spring onions and radish.

BALTI MURGH MAKKAI

Chicken with Corn

Serves: 4

½ kg boneless chicken, cut into 1" pieces
3 tbsp oil
1 tsp ground garlic
1 tsp ground ginger
2 onions, grated
1 cup boiled corn off the cob
1 tsp chilli powder
1 tsp garam masala powder
1 cup fresh tomato purée made from 3 large tomatoes
2 bay leaves (tej patta)
1 tsp salt
2 capsicum, diced

Garnish:

8-10 sprigs basil or tulsi leaves
8-10 sprigs mint leaves

- Heat oil in a non-stick pan and fry garlic, ginger and onions till light brown.

- Add chicken and fry for 10 minutes, stirring constantly.

- Add remaining ingredients except capsicum.

- Cover pan and cook on low heat till chicken is tender.

- Add capsicum and cook for a further 5 minutes.

- Place chicken in a dish and garnish with basil and mint sprigs.

- Serve with naan or roomali roti.

Note: Half a teaspoon thyme or ajwain may be added for extra flavour.

KHUMB SHIMLA MIRCH MURGH KATRI

Chicken with Mushrooms and Capsicum

Serves: 4

½ kg boneless chicken, shredded
3 tbsp oil
1 tsp ground garlic
1 tsp ground ginger
1 tsp chilli powder
1 tsp garam masala powder
¼ tsp turmeric powder
1 tsp salt
2 onions, sliced
1 cup fresh tomato purée, made from 3 large tomatoes
200 gm mushrooms, sliced
2 green capsicums, sliced

Garnish:
Chopped coriander leaves

- Heat oil in a kadahi or wok. Add garlic and ginger, stir and fry till golden brown.
- Add chicken, powdered spices and salt. Fry for 7-8 minutes, stirring continuously.
- Add onion and fry for 5 minutes.
- Stir in tomato purée and fry till oil starts to bubble on top, stirring occasionally.
- Add mushrooms and fry on high heat for 5-6

minutes stirring all the while.

- Mix in capsicum and cook further for 2-3 minutes.

- Place chicken in a dish and garnish with chopped coriander leaves.

- Serve with roomali roti or naan.

KASHMIRI BALTI MURGH SKARDU

Diced Chicken – Kashmir Style

Serves: 4

½ kg boneless chicken, cut into 3" cubes
3 tbsp oil
1 tsp ground garlic
1 tsp ground ginger
3 medium-sized onions, ground
1 tsp sesame seeds (til)
1 tsp poppy seeds (khus khus)
1 tsp aniseed (saunf)
1 tsp seeds of green cardamom
1 tsp chilli powder
1 tsp Kashmiri garam masala powder
1 tsp salt
1 cup cream
½ tsp sugar

- Heat oil in a non-stick kadahi or wok.

- Add garlic, ginger and onions and fry till light brown.

- Mix in sesame seeds, poppy seeds, aniseed and cardamom seeds. Fry for a few seconds.

- Add chicken and fry for 10 minutes, stirring constantly.

- Add chilli powder, garam masala powder, salt and one cup water.

- Simmer for 10 minutes on low heat.
- Stir in cream and sugar. Cook for a further 8-10 minutes.
- Serve with roomali roti or naan.

BALTI MURGH KHARA MASALA

Chicken in Whole Spices

Serves: 4

½ kg boneless chicken, cut into 3" cubes
3 tbsp oil
2 bay leaves (tej patta)
4 green cardamoms
1" piece cinnamon
6-7 cloves
2 dried red chillies
1½ cups curd, beaten till smooth
8-10 cloves of garlic
1 tbsp ginger, sliced
100 gm pickling or button onions
2-3 whole green chillies
1 tbsp chopped coriander leaves
1 tbsp chopped mint leaves
1 tsp chilli powder
1 tsp garam masala powder
1 tsp caraway seeds (shahi jeera)
1 tsp salt
A few strands saffron

Garnish:

3 hard-boiled eggs, cut into quarters

- Heat oil in a non-stick kadahi or wok.
- Add bay leaves, cardamoms, cinnamon, cloves and dried red chillies.
- Fry for a few seconds and add chicken. Fry for a

further 5-6 minutes, stirring continuously.

- Add curd to chicken with remaining ingredients except saffron.

- Cover pan and cook on low heat till chicken is tender and oil starts to bubble on top top.

- Add saffron and simmer for a further 5 minutes.

- Place chicken in a dish and garnish with hard-boiled eggs.

- Serve with naan or roomali roti.

PAKHTOONI MURGH BALTI

Diced Chicken – Pakhtoon Style

Serves: 4

½ kg boneless chicken, cut into 3" cubes
3 tbsp oil
1 tsp caraway seeds (shahi jeera)
2 dried red chillies
1 tsp ground garlic
1 tsp ground ginger
3 onions, ground
1 tsp fenugreek seeds (methi)
1 tsp onion seeds (kalaunji)
1 tsp aniseed (saunf)
1 tsp green cardamom seeds
½ tsp turmeric powder
1 tsp chilli powder
1 tsp garam masala powder
1 tsp salt
50 gm dry figs
50 gm stoned dates
50 gm pine nuts (chilgoza)
1 tbsp honey

- Heat oil in a non-stick kadahi or wok and add caraway seeds and dried red chillies. Stir for a moment and add garlic, ginger and onions. Fry till brown.

- Stir in fenugreek seeds, onion seeds, aniseed and cardamom. Fry for a few seconds.

- Add turmeric powder, chilli powder, garam masala

powder and salt.

- Stir and add chicken. Fry for 10 minutes, stirring continuously.

- Mix in dry fruits, pine nuts, honey and 1½ cups water.

- Simmer on low heat for 20-25 minutes, till chicken is tender and gravy is thick.

- Serve with plain boiled rice, pulao, roomali roti or naan.

AFGHANI ZAFRANI MURG

Chicken with Lamb's Liver and Kidney – Balti Style

Serves: 4-5

½ kg boneless chicken, cut into 1" cubes
¼ kg lamb's liver and kidney, in equal proportion, cut into 1" pieces
3 tbsp oil
2 onions, sliced
3 dried red chillies, kept whole
¼ tsp powdered mace
¼ tsp powdered cinnamon
1 tsp powdered green cardamom
1 tbsp roasted gram flour (besan)
1 tbsp powdered almonds
1 tbsp powdered poppy seeds
1 tbsp powdered dry coconut
¼ tsp saffron
2 tbsp black sultanas (kishmish)

Marinade:

1½ cups thick curd, beaten till smooth
1 tsp ground garlic
1 tsp ground ginger
1 tbsp chopped green chillies
1 tbsp chopped coriander leaves
1 tbsp chopped mint leaves
1½ tsp salt
1 tsp chilli powder
½ tsp turmeric powder

- Mix ingredients for marinade. Add chicken and allow to marinate for 20 minutes.

- Heat oil in a kadahi or wok and fry onions till golden. Remove onions, drain and keep aside.

- Add whole red chillies to pan and fry for 2-3 seconds.

- Add marinated chicken and liver and kidney.

- Cover pan and simmer till chicken is three-quarters cooked.

- Add remaining ingredients, except fried onions.

- Continue frying over low heat for a further 7-8 minutes.

- Place chicken in a dish and garnish with fried onions.

- Serve with naan or roomali roti.

MURGH NIYOZA

Chicken with Pine Nuts

Serves: 4

½ kg boneless chicken, shredded
3 tbsp + 1 tsp oil
1-2 dry red chillies
1 tsp ground garlic
1 tsp ground ginger
1 onion, chopped
½ tsp chilli powder
½ tsp garam masala powder
1 tsp salt

Garnish:

½ cup pine nuts (chilgoza)
½ cup black currants
Sprigs of mint leaves

- Heat 3 tablespoons oil in a non-stick kadahi or wok and lightly fry red chillies.

- Mix in garlic, ginger and onion and fry for 6-7 minutes till light brown.

- Add chicken, powdered spices and salt and fry for 7-8 minutes, stirring occasionally.

- Stir in one cup water and cook on low heat for 8 minutes.

- Heat one teaspoon oil in another pan and fry pine nuts till golden.

- Place chicken in a dish and garnish with pine nuts, black currants and mint leaves.

- Serve with a plain pulao, naan or roomali roti.

Note: Pine nuts may be roasted to a light brown colour in a non-stick pan, to reduce the oil in the dish.

MURGH MUSALLAM

Whole Masala Chicken

Serves: 6-8

Murgh Musallam was a delicacy served to the nobility at the royal court of the Sultanate Empire of Delhi.

1½ kg whole chicken, without skin
2 tsp chilli powder
1½ tsp garam masala powder
Ghee for basting

Marinade:

½ cup curd, beaten till smooth
1 tsp ground garlic
1 tsp ground ginger
2 tsp salt
1 tsp tenderon powder or 1 tbsp ground raw papaya
1 tbsp lime juice

Grind to a paste with a little water:

50 gm dry coconut
50 gm (4 tbsp) sultanas (kishmish)
50 gm (⅓ cup) almonds
¼ tsp saffron

- Make deep cuts in chicken flesh.

- Mix ingredients for marinade, apply onto chicken and allow to marinate for 2 hours.

- Add chilli powder and garam masala to chicken.

- Grease a baking tray with ghee. Apply ground dry fruit paste all over chicken and place it on the tray. Sprinkle ghee over chicken.

- Roast at 200°C (400°F) for 15 minutes. Reduce heat to 180°C (350°F) and continue roasting for a further 20-25 minutes.

- Baste chicken with ghee from the tray occasionally to prevent it from drying.

- Serve with plain pulao.

ZAFRANI BHARWA MURGH

Saffron Flavoured Stuffed Chicken

Serves: 6

Chicken:

1½ kg whole chicken, without skin
3 tsp oil
1 large onion, grated
¾ cup curd, beaten till smooth
1 tsp chilli powder
1 tsp garam masala powder
1 tsp salt
¼ tsp saffron

Marinade:

1 tsp ground garlic
1 tsp ground ginger
1 tbsp lime juice

Filling:

1 tbsp oil
1 onion, chopped
200 gm fresh green gram (hara chana) or green peas
¼ tsp salt
¼ tsp pepper

Garnish:

3 hard-boiled eggs, sliced
Lime slices

Marinade:

- Clean inside of chicken and make gashes in the flesh.

- Mix ingredients for marinade and apply inside and outside of chicken.
- Allow to marinate for half an hour.

Filling:

- Heat oil for filling and fry chopped onion for 5 minutes.
- Add green gram or peas and fry for 5-6 minutes.
- Mix in salt and pepper.

Chicken:

- Stuff filling into chicken cavity. Insert legs of chicken inside cavity and tie with string.
- Heat 3 teaspoons oil in a deep pan. Add grated onion and fry till golden brown.
- Add chicken and fry, turning frequently, till golden on all sides.
- Stir in beaten curd, chilli powder, garam masala powder and salt.
- Cover pan and cook on low heat, turning occasionally till chicken is tender.
- Mix in saffron and cook further for 4-5 minutes.
- Place chicken on a platter and garnish with sliced hard-boiled eggs and lime.

Note: Plain rice pulao can be arranged around the chicken.

MURGH LAJAWAB

Stuffed Chicken Breasts or Legs

Serves: 2

4 chicken breasts or legs
1 egg, lightly beaten
Breadcrumbs as required
Oil for deep frying

Marinade:

2 tsp ground garlic
2 tsp ground ginger
½ tsp chilli powder
½ tsp salt
2 tbsp lime juice

Stuffing:

150 gm hung curd or cream cheese
4 tbsp mint chutney
½ tsp powdered caraway seeds (shahi jeera)
½ tsp salt

Garnish:

Sliced fresh vegetables

- Flatten chicken breast with a blunt chopper, retaining side bone.

- Debone chicken legs keeping the small side bone and flatten with a rolling pin.

- Mix ingredients for marinade and rub onto chicken.

- Marinate for about half an hour to one hour.
- Mix all ingredients for stuffing and divide into 4 portions.
- Place one portion in the centre of each piece of chicken and roll flesh over to cover filling.
- Chill for 15-20 minutes.
- Dip stuffed chicken pieces in beaten egg.
- Roll in breadcrumbs and deep fry in oil.
- Arrange chicken in a dish and garnish with sliced fresh vegetables.

MURGH MAKHANI

Butter Chicken

Serves: 2

Murgh makhani is an all-time favourite, made popular by the chefs of the Moti Mahal Restaurant in Old Delhi, where foreigners intermingled with the local people, and learnt to eat chicken with their hands.

½ kg grilled tandoori chicken, jointed (see recipe)
50 gm (3 tbsp) butter
½ tsp ground garlic
½ tsp ground ginger
1 bay leaf (tej patta)
2 tbsp powdered almonds or cashew nuts
3 cups fresh tomato purée made from 9 large tomatoes
2 tbsp tomato ketchup
¾ tsp chilli powder
¾ tsp garam masala powder
¾ tsp salt

Garnish:

3 tbsp fresh thick cream
Slit green chillies
Chopped coriander leaves

- Melt butter in a non-stick pan and lightly fry garlic and ginger.

- Add bay leaf and powdered nuts.

- Fry on low heat, stirring constantly till golden.

- Add tomato purée, ketchup, powdered spices and salt. Cover pan and cook on medium heat for 8-9 minutes.

- Add chicken and cook for 8-9 minutes further, till gravy is thick.

- Place chicken in a dish and garnish with swirls of cream, green chillies and coriander leaves.

- Serve with naan or roti.

Note: A teaspoon of powdered dry fenugreek leaves (kasuri methi) can be added to the chicken along with the other spices for extra flavour.

ACHARI MURGH

Pickled Chicken

Serves: 2

Achari Murgh originated from the royal family of Bhopal. The spices impart a variety of properties, for example, aniseed helps in digestion, fenugreek is an anti-diabetic, onion seeds reduce water retention and mustard seeds are antiseptic.

It is a mouth-watering dish and leaves a lingering taste of Indian pickle.

½ kg chicken, jointed
3 tbsp oil
1 tsp ground garlic
1 tsp ground ginger
3 medium-sized onions, grated
1 tsp salt
8-10 black peppercorns, coarsely ground
2 bay leaves (tej patta)
1 tbsp mustard oil
2 dried red chillies
1 tsp fenugreek seeds (methi)
1 tsp onion seeds (kalaunji)
¼ tsp powdered asafoetida (hing)
1 tsp mustard seeds
1 tsp aniseed (saunf)
1 tsp garam masala powder
1 tsp chilli powder
½ tsp turmeric powder
1½ cups thick curd, beaten till smooth

- Heat 3 tablespoons oil in a non-stick pan. Add garlic, ginger and onions and fry till onions are crisp and brown. Add chicken, salt, pepper and bay leaves. Fry for 8-9 minutes, stirring constantly.

- Transfer chicken to a deep pan, add one cup water, cover pan and cook on low heat till chicken is tender.

- Heat mustard oil in a non-stick pan till it smokes. Add dried red chillies and reduce heat. Fry for a moment and mix in fenugreek seeds, onion seeds, asafoetida, mustard seeds and aniseed. Fry for a few seconds. Add remaining powdered spices and remove from heat.

- Add beaten curd and mix well.

- Add masala and curd mixture to chicken.

- Cook on low heat for 8-10 minutes till gravy is thick.

- Serve with naan, roti or plain boiled rice.

Note: A teaspoon of flour can be added to the curd to prevent it from curdling.

BADAMI MURGH

Chicken with Almonds

Serves: 4

½ kg boneless chicken, cut into 2" cubes
3 tbsp oil
1 tsp ground garlic
1 tsp ground ginger
2 medium-sized onions, grated
1 tbsp powdered poppy seeds (khus khus)
4 tbsp blanched, peeled and ground almonds
8-10 whole green cardamoms, ground
2 cups milk
½ tsp powdered mace (javitri)
¼ tsp powdered nutmeg
½ tsp garam masala powder
1 tsp salt

Garnish:
A few almonds, blanched, peeled and slivered

- Heat oil in a non-stick pan and lightly fry ginger and garlic.

- Add onions and fry till golden brown.

- Add chicken and fry till golden, stirring frequently.

- Stir in poppy seeds, almonds and cardamom and fry for a few seconds.

- Add milk, mace and nutmeg. Stir and transfer to a deep pan.

- Cook on low heat stirring constantly till gravy thickens. Do not cover pan, else milk will boil and curdle.

- Add garam masala powder and salt and simmer for 5 minutes.

- Place chicken in a dish and garnish with slivered almonds.

- Serve with plain boiled rice.

Note: When cooking with milk, salt should be added towards the end of the cooking process to prevent milk from curdling.

PISTA MURGH

Chicken with Pistachio Nuts

Serves: 6

Pista murgh—the delicate flavour of pistachio combined with chicken—brings back memories of the valleys of Afganistan and Kashmir with their pistachio laden trees.

1 kg chicken breasts
4 tbsp oil
3-4 cloves
3-4 pieces cinnamon, 1" each

Marinade:

6 green cardamoms
1½ tsp cumin seeds
1 green tomato, chopped
1 tbsp chopped coriander leaves
1 tbsp chopped green chillies
1½ tsp ground garlic
1½ tsp ground ginger
1½ tsp salt
1 tsp powdered white pepper
100 gm (¾ cup) pistachio nuts
1 cup curd, beaten till smooth

Garnish:

½ cup thick cream

- Blend all ingredients for marinade and mix with chicken. Allow chicken to marinate for 2 hours.

- Heat oil in a pan and fry cloves and cinnamon for 2-3 minutes.

- Add chicken with marinade. Cover pan and cook on low heat till chicken is tender and gravy is thick.

- Place chicken in a dish and garnish with swirls of cream.

- Serve with naan, roti or plain boiled rice.

KAJU MURGH

Chicken with Cashew Nuts

Serves: 5-6

¾ kg chicken, jointed
3-4 tbsp oil
1 tsp ground garlic
1 tsp ground ginger
2 tomatoes, chopped
100 gm (½ cup) ground cashew nuts
1 cup chopped coriander leaves
1 tbsp chopped green chillies

Marinade:

1 tsp salt
1 tsp garam masala powder
¼ tsp turmeric powder
A pinch of powdered asafoetida (hing)

- Mix ingredients for marinade and rub into chicken.

- Heat oil in a pan and fry chicken for 7-8 minutes, stirring frequently.

- Stir in garlic, ginger, tomatoes and cashew nut and fry till oil starts to bubble on top.

- Add coriander leaves, green chillies and 2 cups water. Cover pan and cook on low heat till chicken is tender. Stir occasionally to ensure that cashew nut does not stick to pan and burn.

- Serve with naan or roti.

NAWABI MURGH

Chicken with Cashew Nuts – Lucknow Style

Serves: 4

½ kg chicken breasts
2+2 tbsp oil
3-4 cloves
2 pieces cinnamon, 1" each
6 green cardamoms
3 onions, grated
50 gm (⅓ cup) blanched almonds
100 gm (⅔ cup) cashew nuts
2 tbsp powdered poppy seeds (khus khus)
1 tsp ground garlic
1 tsp ground ginger
1½ tsp salt
1½ cups thick curd, beaten till smooth
¼ tsp powdered nutmeg
¼ tsp powdered mace

Garnish:

Sliced green chillies

- Heat 2 tablespoons oil in a non-stick pan and fry cloves, cinnamon and cardamom for one minute.

- Add onions and fry for 8-9 minutes, till golden.

- Add almonds and cashew nuts and continue frying for 3-4 minutes, stirring constantly.

- Mix in poppy seeds and fry for a further minute.

- Stir in one cup water and simmer for 10 minutes.

Cool and grind to a smooth paste.

- Heat 2 tablespoons oil in a non-stick pan and fry garlic and ginger for one minute.

- Add chicken and salt and fry, stirring frequently till chicken is golden.

- Add in beaten curd, one cup hot water, ground fried spice paste, nutmeg and mace.

- Mix well, cover pan and simmer on low heat till chicken is tender and gravy is thick.

- Place chicken in a dish and garnish with sliced green chillies.

- Serve with naan or roti.

ANARI AKHROAT MURGH

Chicken with Walnut and Pomegranate

Serves: 4

The Moghul rulers were very conscious of their health and age and the hakims tried to incorporate ingredients considered good for the health in their diet. This was one of the recipes created for them. It includes walnuts, considered good for the heart and pomegranate, considered good for the blood.

1 kg chicken, jointed
3-4 tbsp oil
1 tsp ground garlic
1 onion, grated
¼ tsp turmeric powder
100 gm walnuts, ground
1 tsp garam masala powder
1 tsp chilli powder
1 tsp salt
3 tbsp pomegranate juice

Garnish:

½ cup pomegranate seeds
A few walnuts, chopped

- Heat oil in a non-stick pan and fry chicken till brown. Remove chicken from pan and keep aside.

- Add garlic, onion and turmeric powder to pan. Stir and fry till brown.

- Mix in walnuts, garam masala powder, chilli powder and salt. Fry for 2-3 minutes, stirring continuously.

- Add chicken with 2 cups water.

- Cover pan and cook on low heat till chicken is tender.

- Stir in pomegranate juice and cook for a further 5 minutes.

- Place chicken in a dish and garnish with pomegranate seeds and chopped walnuts.

- Serve with plain boiled rice.

KHURBANI MURGH

Chicken with Apricot

Serves: 4

The Persian influence is very much in evidence in this recipe, where apricots from Afghanistan were used. The combination of apricots with meat is popular amongst the Parsi, Muslim and Kashmiri communities.

½ kg boneless chicken, cut into 3" cubes
3 tbsp oil
3 pieces cinnamon, 1" each
3 green cardamoms
3 cloves
1 tsp ground garlic
1 tsp ground ginger
2 onions, chopped
1 tsp garam masala powder
1 tsp chilli powder
½ tsp turmeric powder
150 gm dry apricots
1 tsp salt

- Heat oil in a non-stick pan and fry whole spices for one minute.

- Add garlic, ginger and onions and fry till brown.

- Add chicken and fry for 8-9 minutes, stirring frequently.

- Stir in powdered spices, apricots, salt and 2½ cups water.

- Cover pan and cook on low heat for 15 minutes till chicken is tender.

- Serve with plain boiled rice.

Note: The apricots may be soaked in water for 1-2 hours and stoned. Add the soaking water, with the apricots to cook the chicken.

MURGH NOORJEHANI

Chicken with Curd and Nuts – Mughlai Style

Serves: 4

1 kg boneless chicken, cut into 2" cubes
4-5 tbsp oil
3 onions, sliced
1 tbsp ground garlic
1 tbsp ground ginger
3 tsp chilli powder
1½ tsp garam masala powder
1½ tsp salt
1 cup curd, beaten till smooth
50 gm (¼ cup) ground cashew nuts or almonds
10-12 whole green cardamoms, ground
¼ tsp saffron
1 tbsp kewra essence
50 gm (¼ cup) khoya (dried condensed milk)

Garnish:

Black sultanas (kishmish)
Sprigs of mint leaves

- Heat oil in a non-stick pan and fry onions till brown and crisp.

- Remove onions from pan and drain.

- Add garlic and ginger to pan and fry for a moment.

- Remove garlic and ginger from pan and drain.

- Crush onions, garlic and ginger with a rolling pin and keep aside.

- Add chicken to pan and fry till golden brown.

- Mix in chilli powder, garam masala powder and salt. Fry for 8-9 minutes, stirring constantly.

- Transfer chicken to a deep pan along with one cup water.

- Cover pan and cook on low heat till chicken is three-quarters done.

- Add beaten curd and mix well. Continue cooking on low heat till chicken is tender.

- Mix in cashew nut and cardamom.

- Add fried ground onion, ginger and garlic.

- Simmer for a further 5 minutes.

- Mix saffron and kewra essence and add to chicken.

- Crumble khoya and roast in a non-stick pan on low heat without oil till pale gold.

- Add to chicken and cook for 5 minutes more stirring constantly.

- Place chicken in a dish and garnish with black sultanas and sprigs of mint leaves.

- Serve with naan or roti.

KHOYA MURGH

Chicken in Dry Condensed Milk

Serves: 4

½ kg boneless chicken, cut into 2" cubes
200 gm (1 cup) khoya (dried condensed milk)
2 tbsp oil
½ tsp ground garlic
½ tsp ground ginger
3 medium-sized onions, grated or ground
1 cup fresh tomato purée, made from 3 large tomatoes
1½ tsp chilli powder
½ tsp garam masala powder
¼ tsp turmeric powder
1½ tsp salt

Garnish:

Chopped coriander leaves

- Lightly roast khoya in a non-stick pan till pale gold.
- Remove and keep aside.
- Add oil to pan, heat and lightly fry garlic and ginger.
- Add onions and fry till light brown.
- Mix in tomato purée and cook till masala is well fried and oil starts to bubble on top.
- Add powdered spices and salt and stir for a moment.
- Mix in chicken and transfer to a deep pan. Stir in 2 cups water.

- Cover pan and cook on low heat for 15-20 minutes.
- Mix in khoya and cook for a further 5 minutes.
- Place chicken in a dish and garnish with chopped coriander leaves.
- Serve with plain boiled rice or naan.

SANDLI MURGH

Saffron Flavoured Chicken

Serves: 6

This recipe for sandli murgh is a special family one and has its origin in Persia and Afghanistan. It is an exotic preparation, and can be made even richer by increasing the quantity of almonds and melon seeds.

1 kg boneless chicken, cut into 3" cubes
3 tbsp ghee or oil
1 tsp ground garlic
1 tsp ground ginger
3 cups milk
1 tsp salt
1 tsp garam masala powder
½ tsp saffron
½ tsp powdered nutmeg
½ tsp powdered mace (javitri)

Grind to a smooth paste:
20 gm (2 tbsp) poppy seeds (khus khus)
20 gm (2 tbsp) char magaz (melon, cucumber and pumpkin seeds)
100 gm (¾ cup) blanched almonds
12 whole green cardamoms

- Heat ghee in a non-stick pan and fry garlic, ginger and chicken till brown.

- Mix in ground paste and fry for 2-3 minutes.

- Transfer to a deep pan and add milk. Cook on low

heat till gravy thickens, stirring all the while to prevent milk from curdling.

- Add in salt, garam masala powder, saffron, nutmeg and mace. Cook till ghee floats on top.

- Serve with plain boiled rice or naan.

MURGH DO PIAZA

Chicken in Onion Gravy

Serves: 2

This dish originated in the royal kitchens of Emperor Akbar, according to the *Ain-I-Akbari*. Edward Terry, in the reign of Jehangir lauded the dish as 'the most savoury dish I have tasted.'

½ kg chicken, jointed
3-4 tbsp oil
1 tsp ground garlic
1 tsp ground ginger
½ kg (4 large) onions, half grated and half sliced
1 tsp chilli powder
1 tsp garam masala powder
¼ tsp turmeric powder
1 tsp salt
1 tbsp chopped green chillies
1 tbsp chopped coriander leaves
1 cup curd

- Heat oil in a non-stick pan and fry garlic, ginger and sliced onions till golden.

- Add chicken and fry for 8-9 minutes, stirring constantly.

- Add powdered spices and salt and fry for a few seconds.

- Mix in green chillies, coriander leaves and curd.

- Add one cup water, cover pan and cook for 20 minutes.
- Stir in grated onions and cook on low heat for 8-10 minutes further.
- Serve with naan or roti.

MURGH ROGAN JOSH

Chicken in Tomato and Curd Gravy

Serves: 4-6

The unusual combination of spices used to prepare rogan josh makes it quite delectable, more so if cooked in a kadahi and served with tandoori roti or naan.

¾ kg boneless chicken, cut into 2" cubes
3 tsp oil
1 tsp ground garlic
1 tsp ground ginger
3 medium-sized onions, grated
1 tsp garam masala powder
1 tsp chilli powder
½ tsp turmeric powder
½ tsp caraway seeds (shahi jeera)
¼ tsp asafoetida (hing)
1 tsp powdered dry ginger (sonth)
1 tsp powdered aniseed (saunf)
1 tsp salt
1½ cups fresh tomato purée, made from 4-5 large tomatoes
¾ cup curd, beaten till smooth

Garnish:

Chopped coriander leaves

- Heat oil in a non-stick pan and fry garlic, ginger and onions till brown.

- Mix in powdered spices and salt and fry for a few seconds.

- Add chicken and fry for 7-8 minutes, stirring occasionally.

- Stir in tomato purée and fry till oil starts to bubble on top.

- Transfer chicken to a deep pan.

- Add one cup water, cover pan and simmer on medium heat for 20 minutes.

- Add beaten curd and cook on low heat for a further 8-10 minutes.

- Place chicken in a dish and garnish with chopped coriander leaves.

- Serve with naan, tandoori roti or parantha.

MURGH ZALFRAZIE

Chicken Curry Laced with Eggs

Serves: 4

½ kg boneless chicken, cut into 2" cubes
3 tbsp oil
1 tsp ground garlic
1 tsp ground ginger
2 medium-sized onions, grated
¾ cup fresh tomato purée made from 2 large tomatoes
1 tsp garam masala powder
1½ tsp chilli powder
½ tsp turmeric powder
1 tsp salt
2 eggs, lightly beaten

- Heat oil in a non-stick pan and fry garlic, ginger and onions till golden brown.

- Add tomato purée and fry till oil starts to bubble on top.

- Mix in dry spices and salt and fry for a moment. Add chicken and continue frying for 6-7 minutes.

- Transfer chicken to a deep pan.

- Add 3 cups water and stir. Cover pan and cook on low heat for 10 minutes.

- Remove pan from heat.

- Gradually add lightly beaten eggs to the hot gravy stirring constantly to attain a lacy effect.

- Place chicken in a dish and serve with naan or roti.

DAL MURGH

Chicken with Lentils

Serves: 6

The combination of dal and meat is popular in most Indian communities.

1 kg chicken, jointed
½ cup pigeon peas (toover or arhar ki dal)
½ cup husked Egyptian lentils (masoor ki dal)
3 tbsp oil
3 onions, grated
1½ tsp ground garlic
1½ tsp ground ginger
1½ tsp chilli powder
1 tsp garam masala powder
½ tsp turmeric powder
1½ tsp salt
1½ cups blanched, peeled and chopped tomatoes
2 tbsp tamarind juice, made with 1 tbsp seedless tamarind, soaked in
4 tbsp water

- Wash dals and cook with 4 cups water on low heat till tender. Purée in a food processor.

- Heat oil in a non-stick pan and fry onions, garlic and ginger till brown.

- Add chicken and fry, stirring constantly till light brown.

- Stir in powdered spices and salt and fry gently for 2-3 minutes.

- Mix in tomatoes and continue frying till oil starts to bubble on top.

- Add 2 cups water and cook till chicken is half done.

- Mix in dal purée and cook further till chicken is tender.

- Strain tamarind juice into pan. Mix well and cook further for 5-6 minutes.

- Serve with plain boiled rice.

MURGH KOFTA

Chicken Meatball Curry

Serves: 4

Kofta:

½ kg chicken mince
1 onion, chopped
1 tsp ground garlic
1 tsp ground ginger
1 tbsp chopped green chillies
1 tbsp chopped coriander leaves
1 tbsp chopped mint leaves
1 tsp chilli powder
1 tsp garam masala powder
1 tsp salt
2 slices bread, crusts removed if desired
2 eggs, lightly beaten
Oil for deep frying

Gravy:

2 tbsp oil
3 cloves
3 pieces cinnamon, 1" each
2 bay leaves (tej patta)
1 tsp ground garlic
1 tsp ground ginger
1 onion, grated
1 tsp chilli powder
¼ tsp powdered mace
¼ tsp powdered nutmeg
½ tsp powdered green cardamom seeds
1 tsp salt

Main Course Dishes   97

1½ cups thick curd, beaten till smooth

Garnish:

Mint leaves

- Mix all ingredients for kofta, except oil.

- Divide into 16 portions.

- Shape into round balls and deep fry in hot oil till brown.

- Heat oil for gravy in a non-stick kadahi or wok. Add cloves, cinnamon, bay leaves and fry for a few seconds. Add garlic, ginger and grated onion and fry till light brown.

- Mix in powdered spices, salt and beaten curd. Cover pan and simmer on low heat for 10 minutes.

- Gently add koftas and cook for 5 minutes.

- Place curry in a dish, taking care not to break koftas.

- Garnish with mint leaves and serve with plain boiled rice or naan.

SHIKAMPURI MURGH KOFTA

Stuffed Chicken Meatball Curry

Serves: 6

The recipe is an innovated one and the dish is delicious!

Kofta:

¾ kg chicken mince
1 tsp ground garlic
1 large onion, grated
½ tsp chilli powder
1 tsp garam masala powder
2 tbsp Bengal gram (chané ki dal)
½ tsp salt
1 egg, lightly beaten
Oil for deep frying

Filling:

200 gm (¾ cup) hung curd or cream cheese
2 tbsp ground mint leaves
1 tsp salt
1 tsp pepper

Gravy:

1½ cups grated coconut
3 tbsp oil
1 tsp ground garlic
1 tsp ground ginger
1 onion, grated
2 tsp powdered coriander seeds
2 tsp powdered cumin seeds

Main Course Dishes

1 tsp garam masala powder
1 tsp chilli powder
¼ tsp turmeric powder
1 tsp salt
2 bay leaves (tej patta)

Garnish:

Chopped mint leaves

Kofta:

- Place all ingredients for kofta, except egg and oil, in a pan with three-quarter cup water and cook on low heat till dry. Grind to a smooth paste and mix in egg.

- Mix all ingredients for filling.

- Divide ground mince into 16 portions.

- Flatten each portion into a round disc. Place 2 teaspoons filling on each disc. Work mince around to cover filling and shape into round balls.

- Deep fry stuffed koftas in oil, till light brown.

Gravy:

- Blend coconut for gravy with 3 cups hot water in a liquidizer or food processor. Strain and reserve coconut milk.

- Heat oil in a non-stick pan and fry garlic, ginger and onion till brown.

- Mix in powdered spices, salt, bay leaves and coconut milk. Cook on low heat for 20 minutes, stirring constantly.

- Gently add koftas.

- Place curry in a dish, taking care not to break koftas.

- Garnish with mint leaves and serve with plain boiled rice or naan.

NARGISI MURGH KOFTA CURRY

Scotch Eggs – Mughlai Style

Serves: 4

Kofta:

½ kg chicken mince
2 tbsp Bengal gram (chané ki dal)
1 medium-sized onion, grated
1 tsp ground ginger
1 tsp ground garlic
½ tsp salt
½ tsp chilli powder
1 tbsp chopped coriander leaves
2 green chillies, chopped
½ tsp garam masala powder
1 egg, lightly beaten
8 hard-boiled eggs
Oil for deep frying

Gravy:

2 tbsp oil
½ tsp ground garlic
½ tsp ground ginger
1 medium-sized onion, grated
1 tsp chilli powder
¼ tsp garam masala powder
1 tsp salt
2 tsp ground cashew nut
2 tsp powdered poppy seeds (khus khus)
1 tbsp ground dry coconut
¾ cup fresh tomato purée, made from 2-3 large tomatoes
¼ tsp saffron

Garnish:

4 tbsp thick cream
Silver leaf (varak)

Kofta:

- Wash mince and dal.

- Place first seven ingredients for kofta in a pressure cooker with half cup water. Mix well and cook under pressure for 8 minutes.

- Allow cooker to cool before removing pressure.

- Place cooker on medium heat and dry out liquid.

- Add coriander leaves, green chillies and garam masala powder. Mix well and grind to a paste.

- Mix in beaten egg.

- Divide mixture into 8 portions.

- Flatten one portion into a disc. Place a hard-boiled egg in the centre. Work mince around egg to cover completely. Make remaining kofta in the same way.

- Deep fry in hot oil till brown, and keep aside.

Gravy:

- Heat oil for gravy in a non-stick pan. Add garlic and ginger and fry lightly. Add onion and fry till golden brown.

- Mix in powdered spices and salt and fry for one minute.

- Add ground cashew nut, poppy seeds and coconut and fry for a few seconds.

Main Course Dishes　　**103**

- Add tomato purée and fry till oil starts to bubble on top.

- Transfer to a deep pan. Add 1½ cups water, cover pan and cook on medium heat for 12-15 minutes. The gravy should have a thick flowing consistency.

- Add in saffron and stir.

- Cut koftas in half lengthwise and place gently in hot gravy, egg side up.

- Transfer to a dish, taking care not to break koftas.

- Garnish with swirls of cream and silver leaf.

- Serve with plain boiled rice or naan.

YAKHANI KASHMIRI MURGH

Chicken Curry – Kashmir Style

Serves: 2

½ kg chicken, jointed
3-4 tbsp oil
1 tsp ground garlic
3 medium-sized onions, grated or ground
3-4 cloves
3-4 pieces cinnamon, 1" each
3-4 whole black peppercorns
1 tsp salt
1 tsp Kashmiri garam masala powder
1 tbsp powdered dry ginger (sonth)
2 tsp powdered aniseed (saunf)
¼ tsp powdered asafoetida (hing)
1½ cups thick curd, beaten till smooth

Garnish:

Sliced green chillies
½ tsp caraway seeds (shahi jeera)

- Heat oil in a non-stick pan and lightly fry garlic.

- Add onions and fry till pale gold.

- Add chicken, cloves, cinnamon and peppercorn and fry for 7-8 minutes.

- Mix in salt, garam masala powder, dry ginger, aniseed and asafoetida. Stir for a moment.

- Add beaten curd and mix well.

- Cover pan and cook on low heat till chicken is tender and gravy is of a thick flowing consistency.

- Place chicken in a dish and garnish with sliced green chillies and caraway seeds.

- Serve with plain boiled rice.

KASHMIRI MURGH ROGAN JOSH

Chicken in Tomato and Curd Gravy – Kashmir Style

Serves: 3-4

As in the case of most Indian dishes, rogan josh today has many variations. The original Kashmiri rogan josh as made by the Hindu Kashmiris consisted of meat fried in ghee with spices and curd, and coloured with dried coxcomb flowers, which also has cooling properties. The Muslims started adding garlic and onions and the Moghuls finally influenced the dish so that it became a combination of curd, tomato and Kashmiri spices.

I have combined the traditional Hindu and Muslim styles of preparing this dish, to enhance the flavour and taste of the chicken, and have been teaching this dish for the last 30 years.

700 gm chicken, jointed
4 tbsp oil
1 tsp ground garlic
2 medium-sized onions, grated or ground
¼ tsp powdered asafoetida (hing)
1 tsp Kashmiri garam masala powder
1 tbsp powdered dry ginger (sonth)
1½ tsp aniseed (saunf)
1 tsp poppy seeds (khus khus)
1½ tsp chilli powder
½ tsp turmeric powder
1 tsp salt
1 cup fresh tomato purée, made from 3 large tomatoes
1 cup thick curd, beaten till smooth

1 tbsp chopped coriander leaves
1 tbsp chopped green chillies
1 tbsp dry fenugreek leaves (kasuri methi)

Garnish:

2 tbsp sultanas
2 tbsp almonds, blanched, peeled and slivered

- Heat oil in a pan and lightly fry garlic.

- Add onions and fry till golden brown.

- Add chicken and fry, turning constantly till pale gold.

- Add all powdered spices and salt. Stir and fry for a few seconds.

- Stir in tomato purée and continue cooking till oil starts to bubble on top.

- Add in one cup water, beaten curd, coriander leaves, green chillies and fenugreek leaves.

- Cover pan and cook on low heat till chicken is tender and gravy is thick.

- Place chicken in a dish and garnish with sultanas and almonds.

- Serve with naan.

KASHMIRI MURGH–GOSHTABA MASALA

Chicken Meatballs in Curd Gravy

Serves: 5-6

To achieve the silky texture of these koftas is the ultimate perfection of skill, and this curry is unmatched by any other kofta curry.

Kofta:

¾ kg chicken mince
2 eggs, lightly beaten
1 tsp salt
2 tbsp powdered dry ginger (sonth)
3 tbsp powdered aniseed (saunf)
1 tsp ground garlic
1 tsp ground ginger
Seeds of 4-5 green cardamoms
12 dry apricots, stoned and chopped
3 tbsp oil
¼ tsp asafoetida (hing)
2 bay leaves (tej patta)
1 tsp caraway seeds (shahi jeera)
½ kg (2¼ cups) curd, beaten till smooth
1 tbsp Kashmiri garam masala powder
¼ tsp saffron

- Mix minced chicken with eggs, half teaspoon salt, one teaspoon dry ginger powder, one teaspoon aniseed powder, ground garlic, ground ginger and cardamom seeds.

- Grind to a smooth paste.

- Divide mixture into egg-size portions.

- Flatten each portion into a disc. Place a little apricot on each disc and work mince around apricot to shape into a ball.

- Bring 3 cups water to boil in a pan.

- Gently immerse koftas and boil for 8-9 minutes.

- Remove koftas carefully from pan, drain and keep aside. Retain half cup water.

- Heat oil in another pan and add asafoetida, bay leaves and caraway seeds. Fry for a few seconds.

- Mix in beaten curd, garam masala and remaining salt, dry ginger powder and aniseed powder. Stir and cook till gravy comes to boil.

- Carefully add koftas with reserved water and saffron. Cover pan and simmer on low heat till gravy is thick.

- Serve with plain boiled rice.

KASHMIRI KALMI – KARBARGAH MASALA

Chicken Drumsticks – Kashmir Style

Serves: 2-3

½ kg chicken drumsticks
¼ litre milk
1½ tsp powdered dry ginger (sonth)
1 tbsp powdered aniseed (saunf)
½ tsp chilli powder
2-3 cloves
2-3 pieces cinnamon, 1" each
2-3 green cardamoms
1 cup thick curd, beaten till smooth
½ tsp salt
½ tsp powdered caraway seed (shahi jeera)
½ tsp Kashmiri garam masala powder
Oil for shallow frying

- Wash chicken drumsticks.
- Place chicken in a pan with milk, dry ginger, aniseed, chilli powder and whole spices and cook till chicken is tender and liquid has evaporated. Cool.
- Whip curd with salt, caraway seed powder and garam masala powder in a bowl.
- Dip chicken into curd mixture and shallow fry till golden brown.
- Serve with mint and walnut chutney.

KALI MIRCH MURGH

Chicken Curry with Black Pepper

Serves: 4

½ kg boneless chicken, cut into 2" cubes
1 tbsp oil
3 cloves
3 green cardamoms
1 bay leaf (tej patta)
1 cup thick curd
1 tbsp powdered black peppercorn
1 tsp salt
1 tsp ground garlic
1 tsp ground ginger
½ tsp garam masala powder
2 tbsp ground cashew nut

Garnish:

Sprigs of mint leaves

- Heat oil in a heavy based deep pan or non-stick pan.

- Add cloves, cardamoms and bay leaf. Fry for a few seconds.

- Add remaining ingredients except powdered cashew nut.

- Cover pan and simmer on low heat till chicken is tender.

- Add ground cashew nut, stir and cook for a further 7-8 minutes.

- Place chicken in a dish and garnish with sprigs of mint leaves.
- Serve with naan or parantha.

KADAHI MURGH

Fried Chicken in Tomato Gravy

Serves: 2

½ kg chicken, jointed
3 tbsp oil
1 tsp ground garlic
1 tsp ground ginger
3 medium-sized onions, grated
1 tsp garam masala powder
1½ tsp chilli powder
½ tsp turmeric powder
1 tsp salt
1 cup fresh tomato purée made from 3 large tomatoes
3 medium-sized potatoes, cut into halves, lengthwise

Garnish:

Sliced green chillies
Chopped coriander leaves
1 tbsp powdered dry fenugreek leaves (kasuri methi)

- Heat oil in a non-stick kadahi or wok and lightly fry garlic and ginger.

- Add onions and fry till brown.

- Stir in powdered spices and salt and fry for a moment. Add chicken and fry till golden brown.

- Add tomato purée and continue frying till oil starts to bubble on top.

- Add potatoes and fry for a further minute.

- Stir in 1½ cups water, cover pan and cook on low heat stirring occasionally till chicken is tender and gravy is thick.

- Place chicken in a dish, garnish with sliced green chillies and chopped coriander leaves and sprinkle with powdered dry fenugreek leaves.

- Serve with naan, tandoori roti or parantha.

MURGH PALAK

Chicken with Spinach

Serves: 2

½ kg chicken, jointed
3 tbsp oil
1 tsp ground garlic
1 tsp ground ginger
3 onions, grated
1 cup fresh tomato purée, made from 3 large tomatoes
1 tsp garam masala powder
1 tsp chilli powder
½ tsp turmeric powder
1 tsp salt
1½ cups boiled, ground spinach

Garnish:

3 tbsp thick fresh cream or milk

- Heat oil in a non-stick pan and lightly fry garlic and ginger.

- Add onions and fry till light brown.

- Stir in tomato purée and fry till oil starts to bubble on top.

- Mix in powdered spices and salt. Fry for a few seconds and add chicken. Fry for 10 minutes more, stirring frequently.

- Transfer chicken to a deep pan with one cup water.

- Cover pan and simmer on low heat for 25 minutes

till chicken is tender.

- Add ground spinach and cook for a further 8-9 minutes.
- Place chicken in a dish and garnish with swirls of cream or milk.
- Serve with naan or roti.

MURGH METHI

Chicken with Fenugreek

Serves: 4

½ kg chicken, jointed
1 cup fresh fenugreek leaves (methi), finely chopped
1 cup dry fenugreek leaves (kasuri methi)
3 tbsp oil
1 tsp ground garlic
1 tsp ground ginger
2 onions, grated
¼ tsp powdered asafoetida (hing)
1 tsp chilli powder
1 tsp garam masala powder
½ tsp turmeric powder
1 tsp salt
1 cup fresh tomato purée, made from 3 large tomatoes

- Mix quarter teaspoon salt with fresh fenugreek leaves and let it stand for 10 minutes. Squeeze out water.

- Soak dry fenugreek leaves in one cup water for 15 minutes.

- Heat oil in a non-stick pan and lightly fry garlic and ginger.

- Add onions and fry till golden brown.

- Add chicken and fry till light brown.

- Stir in powdered spices and remaining salt and fry for a few seconds.

- Add tomato purée and fry till oil starts to bubble on top.

- Mix in dry fenugreek leaves with soaking water along with fresh fenugreek leaves. Add one cup water, cover pan and cook till chicken is tender and oil starts to bubble on top.

- Serve with naan or roti.

Note: 2 tablespoons beaten curd may be added towards the end, to mellow down the bitterness of the fenugreek.

SABZ MURGH

Chicken in Green Herbs

Serves: 2

½ kg chicken, jointed
3 tbsp oil
1 tsp ground garlic
1 tsp ground ginger
3 medium-sized onions, grated or ground

Marinade:

1 cup thick curd, beaten till smooth
1 cup chopped coriander leaves
½ cup chopped spinach leaves
2 tbsp chopped fenugreek leaves (methi)
2 tbsp chopped mint leaves
6-7 green chillies, chopped
1 tsp garam masala powder
½ tsp chilli powder
¼ tsp turmeric powder
1 tsp salt

- Blend curd for marinade with next 5 ingredients in a liquidizer or food processor to a smooth paste.

- Add in dry spices and salt. Mix well.

- Add chicken to marinade and allow to marinate for half an hour.

- Heat oil in a non-stick pan and lightly fry garlic and ginger.

- Add onions and fry till light brown.

- Transfer to a deep pan and add chicken with marinade.

- Cover pan and cook on low heat, till chicken is tender and oil starts to bubble on top.

- Serve with naan or roti.

Note: For fat-free sabz murgh, omit oil. Add ginger, garlic and onion to marinade. Cook marinated chicken on low heat till chicken is tender and gravy is thick.

HARA CHANA MURGH

Chicken with Fresh Green Gram

Serves: 4

This recipe is a family innovation and produces a delicious chicken dish with an unusual taste.

½ kg boneless chicken, cut into 3" cubes
3 tbsp oil
3 onions, grated
1 tsp ground garlic
1 tsp ground ginger
1 tsp chilli powder
½ tsp turmeric powder
½ tsp garam masala powder
1 tsp salt
200 gm fresh green gram (hara chana)
¾ cup fresh tomato purée made from 2 large tomatoes

Garnish:
Chopped coriander leaves
Chopped mint leaves

- Heat oil in a non-stick pan and fry onions, garlic and ginger till light brown.

- Add chicken and fry till light brown, stirring frequently.

- Mix in powdered spices, salt and gram and fry for 5 minutes, stirring occasionally.

- Add tomato purée and cook till spices are well fried

and oil starts to bubble on top.

- Stir in one cup water, cover pan and cook on low heat till chicken is tender and gravy is thick.

- Place chicken in a dish and garnish with chopped coriander and mint leaves.

- Serve with naan, roti or plain boiled rice.

MURGH KEEMA MATAR

Minced Chicken with Green Peas

Serves: 4

½ kg chicken mince
1 cup shelled green peas
3 tbsp oil
1 tsp ground garlic
1 tsp ground ginger
2 medium-sized onions, grated
1 tsp chilli powder
1 tsp garam masala powder
¼ tsp turmeric powder
1 tsp salt
¾ cup fresh tomato purée, made from 2-3 large tomatoes

Garnish:

Chopped mint or coriander leaves

- Heat oil in a non-stick pan and lightly fry garlic and ginger.

- Add onions and fry till light brown.

- Add chicken mince and fry till light brown, stirring constantly.

- Mix in powdered spices and salt and fry for a few seconds.

- Stir in tomato purée and cook till oil starts to bubble on top.

- Add peas and cook for a further for 5-6 minutes.

- Transfer chicken to a deep pan.

- Stir in one cup water, cover pan and cook on low heat for 20-25 minutes.

- Place chicken in a dish and garnish with chopped mint or coriander leaves.

- Serve with roti or plain boiled rice.

PAHADI KHATTI KUKARDI

Chicken in Sour gravy – Kangra Style

Serves: 2

Pahadi or hill sour curries are a speciality of Himachal Pradesh. This thick sour spicy chicken curry and rice make a special Sunday treat.

½ kg chicken, jointed
2 tbsp rice
4 tbsp mustard oil
3 cloves
3 black peppercorns
3 bay leaves (tej patta)
1 tsp ground garlic
1 tsp ground ginger
3 onions, grated
2 tbsp dry mango powder (amchur)
1½ tsp chilli powder
1 tsp garam masala powder
1½ tsp salt

- Soak rice in half cup water for half an hour and grind to a paste.

- Heat mustard oil in a non-stick pan, to smoking point.

- Reduce heat, add whole spices and bay leaves. Toss for a few seconds, and add garlic, ginger and onions. Fry till onions are brown.

- Add chicken and fry till brown, turning chicken

around frequently.

- Mix in dry mango powder and continue frying for 2-3 minutes.

- Add chilli powder, garam masala powder and salt. Stir and add 3 cups water. Cover pan and cook on low heat till chicken is tender.

- Add rice paste and cook further on low heat for 10 minutes.

- Serve with plain boiled rice.

PAHADI MADRA MURGH

Chicken with Curd – Kangra Style

Serves: 4

Frying the curd before adding the chicken imparts a very tasty, grainy texture to this dish.

½ kg boneless chicken, cut into 2" cubes
3-4 tbsp oil
1 tsp ground garlic
1 tsp ground ginger
3-4 cloves
3 green cardamoms
1" piece cinnamon
1 tsp coriander seeds
2 bay leaves (tej patta)
1 kg (4 cups) thick curd, beaten till smooth
½ tsp turmeric powder
1 tsp chilli powder
1 tsp salt
1 tsp garam masala powder

Garnish:

Chopped mint leaves

- Heat oil in a non-stick pan and fry garlic, ginger and chicken till light brown. Remove chicken from pan, drain and keep aside.

- Transfer oil to a large pan and fry cloves, cardamoms, cinnamon, coriander seeds and bay leaves for one minute.

- Reduce heat and add beaten curd, turmeric powder and chilli powder, stirring constantly. Continue cooking till mixture resembles soft granules, and is reddish-yellow.

- Add chicken, salt, garam masala powder and one cup hot water.

- Cover pan and cook for 20 minutes till chicken is tender and oil starts to bubble on top.

- Place chicken in a dish and garnish with chopped mint leaves.

- Serve with plain boiled rice or roti.

PAHADI CHHAACH MURGH

Chicken in Curd – Chamba Style

Serves: 4

This dish is a speciality of Mrs Raj Mahajan.

½ kg chicken, jointed
3 tbsp oil
1 tsp ground garlic
1 tsp ground ginger
4 cloves
4 black peppercorns
4 black cardamoms
1 tsp coriander seeds
3 dry red chillies
1½ tsp chilli powder
1 tsp garam masala powder
1½ tsp salt
1 cup curd, beaten till smooth
3 tbsp gram flour (besan)

Garnish:

Chopped coriander leaves

- Heat oil in a non-stick pan and fry garlic, ginger, cloves, peppercorns, cardamom, coriander seeds and dry chillies for 2-3 minutes.

- Add chicken and fry for 10 minutes, turning frequently.

- Stir in chilli powder, garam masala powder, salt and

one cup water. Cover pan and cook on low heat till chicken is three-quarters done.

- Whisk together, curd, gram flour and 3 cups water.

- Add to chicken. Cook on low heat for about 20 minutes, stirring constantly till gravy thickens slightly.

- Place chicken in a dish and garnish with chopped coriander leaves.

- Serve with plain boiled rice.

MURGHI NARCOLE RANNA

Chicken Curry with Coconut – Bengal Style

Serves: 2

½ kg chicken without skin, jointed
4 tbsp mustard oil
1 tsp ground garlic
1 tsp ground ginger
2 onions, grated
1 tsp chilli powder
½ tsp turmeric powder
2 bay leaves (tej patta)
1 tsp salt
3 cups coconut milk, extracted from 1 large coconut

Garnish:

Sliced green chillies

- Heat oil in a non-stick pan and fry garlic, ginger and onions till light brown.

- Add chicken and fry for 10 minutes, stirring frequently.

- Mix in powdered spices, bay leaves and salt. Stir for a few seconds and add coconut milk.

- Cover pan and cook on low heat for 20-25 minutes till chicken is tender.

- Place chicken in a dish and garnish with sliced green chillies.

MURGHI GOTA MASHLA

Chicken with whole spices – Bengal Style

Serves: 2

½ kg chicken, jointed
3 tbsp oil
4 dry red chillies
6 pieces cinnamon, 1" each
6 cloves
6 black peppercorns
6 green cardamoms
2-3 bay leaves (tej patta)
1 tsp cumin seeds
1 cup curd, beaten till smooth
2 tbsp sliced garlic
2 tbsp sliced ginger
3 medium-sized onions, sliced
1 tsp salt
¼ tsp saffron

Garnish:

Sprigs of mint leaves

- Heat oil in a non-stick pan and add next 7 ingredients. Fry for one minute, stirring constantly.

- Add remaining ingredients, except saffron.

- Cover pan and cook on low heat till chicken is tender and oil starts to bubble on top.

- Add saffron, stir and cook for a further 5 minutes.

- Place chicken in a dish and garnish with mint leaves.

SARSHE MURGHI

Chicken in Mustard Gravy – Bengal Style

Serves: 4

This recipe has been adapted from the famous Bengal fish curry cooked with mustard. It produces a chicken curry, which is deliciously pungent.

You may reduce the quantity of mustard for a milder flavour.

½ kg boneless chicken, cut into 3" cubes
3 tbsp mustard oil
1 cup fresh tomato purée, made from 3 large tomatoes
1 tsp salt
1 tbsp lime juice

Grind to a fine paste:

1 onion
1 tsp ground garlic
1 tsp ground ginger
1 tbsp grated fresh coconut
3 tbsp powdered mustard seeds
3 tbsp powdered poppy seeds (khus khus)
1½ tsp chilli powder
1 tsp cumin powder
½ tsp turmeric powder

Garnish:

Chopped coriander leaves

- Heat oil in a non-stick kadahi or wok and fry

ground masala for 7-8 minutes.

- Add chicken and fry for 8-9 minutes, stirring frequently.

- Mix in tomato purée and salt and cook for 6 minutes.

- Transfer chicken to a deep pan, add 2 cups water, cover pan and simmer on low heat for 20 minutes till chicken is tender.

- Place chicken in a dish sprinkle over lime juice and garnish with coriander leaves.

- Serve with plain boiled rice.

MURGH MAKKAI

Chicken with Corn

Serves: 4

½ kg boneless chicken, cut into 3" cubes
3 tbsp oil
2 onions, grated
½ tsp cumin seeds
3-4 green cardamoms
3-4 cloves
3-4 pieces cinnamon, 1" each
3-4 bay leaves (tej patta)
2 cups fresh corn, grated
1 cup milk

Marinade:

¾ cup curd, beaten till smooth
1 tbsp ground garlic
1 tbsp chopped green chillies
1 tbsp chopped coriander leaves
1 tsp garam masala powder
1 tsp chilli powder
1 tsp coriander powder
¼ tsp turmeric powder
1 tsp salt

Garnish:

Lime slices

- Mix ingredients for marinade, add to chicken and marinate for half an hour.

- Heat oil in a non-stick pan and fry onions till golden brown.

- Add cumin seeds, whole spices and bay leaves and fry for 2-3 minutes.

- Add marinated chicken and mix well.

- Cover pan and simmer on low heat till chicken is three-quarters cooked.

- Mix in corn and milk.

- Cook on low heat for about 10-12 minutes, till gravy is thick, stirring continuously to prevent it from boiling.

- Place chicken in a dish, garnish with lime slices and serve with tandoori roti or parantha.

KHAD MURGH KEEMA

Baked Chicken Mince

Serves: 4

A preparation of it's own kind, it reminds one of Mexican cuisine. It is a Rajasthani speciality and is traditionally baked in a sand pit.

½ kg chicken mince
3 tbsp oil
2 tsp ground garlic
2 tsp ground ginger
3 onions, grated
3 potatoes, peeled and diced
1 tsp garam masala powder
1 tsp chilli powder
¼ tsp turmeric powder
1 tsp salt
½ cup curd, beaten till smooth
1 tbsp chopped green chillies
1 tbsp chopped coriander leaves
8 thin roti

- Heat oil in a non-stick pan and fry garlic, ginger and onions till light brown.

- Add mince and fry till golden brown.

- Add potatoes and fry till golden.

- Stir in powdered spices, salt and curd.

- Cover pan and cook on low heat till oil starts to bubble on top.

- Remove from heat and mix in green chillies and coriander leaves.

- Divide mince into 7 portions.

- Arrange alternate layers of roti and mince, starting and ending with roti.

- Wrap in foil and bake at 180°C (350°F) for 15-20 minutes.

- Slice and serve with mint chutney and a fresh salad or kachumber.

RAJASTHANI SUFAID MURGH

White Chicken Curry – Rajasthan Style

Serves: 2

½ kg chicken, jointed
3 tbsp oil
1 cup curd, beaten till smooth
1 tbsp ground ginger
½ tsp ground green chillies
1 tsp salt
1 tsp powdered white pepper
1 tsp powdered green cardamom
25 gm (about 20) blanched ground almonds
20 gm ground dry coconut
½ cup cream
A few drops kewra or rose essence

- Heat oil in a pan and lightly fry chicken.

- Mix in beaten curd, ginger, green chillies, salt, pepper and cardamom.

- Cover pan and cook on low heat till chicken is tender.

- Mix in ground almonds and coconut.

- Cook on low heat for 5-6 minutes, stirring constantly.

- Remove from heat, add cream and essence. Stir and serve immediately with roti.

RAJASTHANI LAL MURGH

Chicken in Red Gravy – Rajasthan Style

Serves: 4

½ kg boneless chicken, cut into 3" cubes
3 tbsp oil
1 tbsp ground garlic
2 onions, ground
3 green cardamoms
3 black cardamoms
3 cloves
3 pieces cinnamon, 1" each
1½ tsp coriander powder
¼ tsp turmeric powder
12-14 dried red chillies, broken into small pieces
1 tsp cumin seeds
1 tsp salt
½ cup curd, beaten till smooth

Garnish:

1 tbsp chopped coriander leaves

- Heat oil in a non-stick pan and lightly fry garlic. Add onions and fry till brown.

- Add chicken and whole spices and fry for 8-9 minutes, stirring constantly.

- Add remaining ingredients except curd, and fry for one minute.

- Add beaten curd. Stir and cook for 7-8 minutes.

- Stir in 1½ cups hot water. Cover pan and cook on

low heat till chicken is tender.

- Place chicken in a dish and garnish with coriander leaves.
- Serve with roti and papad.

SEYAL MURGH

Chicken Curry with Onions and Green Herbs – Sindhi Style

Serves: 4

In the Sindhi language, *seyal*, means cooking a dish with onions and herbs, and flavoured with spices.

1 kg chicken, jointed
4-5 tbsp oil
5 onions, grated
2 tsp ground garlic
2 tsp ground ginger
2 tsp cumin powder
2 tsp chilli powder
1 tsp garam masala powder
½ tsp turmeric powder
½ tsp powdered mace
1½ tsp salt
3 tomatoes, chopped

Marinade:

1 cup curd, beaten till smooth
1 cup chopped coriander leaves
1 tbsp chopped green chillies

Garnish:

1 tsp powdered caraway seeds (shahi jeera)
1 tsp powdered green cardamom

- Mix ingredients for marinade. Rub into chicken and allow to marinate for half an hour.

- Heat oil in a non-stick pan, and fry onions for 10 minutes, till light brown. Mix in garlic and ginger and fry for 3-4 minutes.

- Add next 6 ingredients, stir and fry for a few seconds. Stir in tomatoes and fry till oil starts to bubble on top.

- Transfer tomato mixture to a deep pan and add chicken. Cover pan and simmer on low heat till chicken is three-quarters cooked. Add one cup hot water and cook further till chicken is tender.

- Place chicken in a dish and sprinkle over caraway seeds and cardamom powder.

- Serve with roti.

SINDHI ELAICHI MURGH

Cardamom Flavoured Chicken – Sindhi Style

Serves: 4

1 kg chicken, jointed
4 tbsp oil
Seeds of 20 green cardamoms, ground
½ tsp freshly ground black pepper
1½ tsp salt
1 tsp chilli powder
2 tsp coriander powder
1 tsp turmeric powder
1 tbsp chopped green chillies
2 tomatoes, chopped
1 cup curd, beaten till smooth

Garnish:

1 tsp powdered caraway seeds (shahi jeera)
Chopped coriander leaves

- Heat oil in a pan and lightly fry ground cardamoms and black pepper.

- Mix in chicken, salt, chilli powder, coriander powder, turmeric powder and green chillies. Fry for 10 minutes.

- Add tomatoes and fry for a further 8-9 minutes.

- Mix in beaten curd and 1½ cups water. Cover pan and cook on low heat till chicken is tender.

- Place chicken in a dish and garnish with powdered caraway seeds and chopped coriander leaves.

- Serve with roti.

SINDHI HARA MURGH

Chicken in Green Curry – Sindhi Style

Serves: 4

1 kg chicken, jointed
3 tbsp oil
1 tsp coriander powder
¼ tsp turmeric powder
1 tsp salt
3 tomatoes, grated

Grind to a paste:

1 cup chopped coriander leaves
1 tsp chopped ginger
10-12 cloves, garlic
5-6 green chillies

- Heat oil in a pan and fry ground paste for 5 minutes, stirring continuously.

- Add in powdered spices, salt and tomatoes and fry till oil starts to bubble on top.

- Add chicken and fry for 7-8 minutes. Stir in 3 cups water, cover pan and cook on low heat till chicken is tender.

- Serve with plain boiled rice.

SINDHI METHI MURGH

Chicken with Fenugreek Leaves – Sindhi Style

Serves: 4

1 kg chicken, jointed
4-5 tbsp oil
3-4 cloves
3-4 black peppercorns
3-4 pieces cinnamon, 1" each
3-4 black cardamoms
10 green cardamoms
2 onions, chopped
2 tsp ground green chillies
2 tsp ground garlic
2 tsp ground ginger
2 tsp coriander powder
1 tsp garam masala powder
5 tomatoes, chopped
1½ cups chopped fenugreek leaves (methi)
1½ tsp salt

- Heat 3 tbsp oil in a non-stick pan, add whole spices and fry for 5 minutes, stirring constantly.

- Mix in onions, green chillies, garlic and ginger and fry for 8-9 minutes.

- Add chicken and fry till brown, stirring frequently.

- Stir in powdered spices and continue frying for 5 minutes.

- Add tomatoes and fry till oil starts to bubble on top.

- Stir in 2 cups water, cover pan and cook on low heat

till chicken is tender.

- Heat remaining oil in a non-stick pan and fry fenugreek leaves, on very low heat for 10 minutes. Add to chicken. Cook further for 8-9 minutes.

- Serve with roti.

BOHRI MURGH

Chicken Curry – Bohra Style

Serves: 2

½ kg chicken, jointed
4 tbsp oil
3-4 cloves
2 pieces cinnamon, 1" each
5-6 black peppercorns
10 curry leaves
200 gm (2 medium-sized) potatoes, cut in quarters
3 onions, chopped
1 tsp ground garlic
1 tsp ground ginger
½ tsp, turmeric powder
½ tsp garam masala powder
1 tsp salt
2 tbsp tamarind soaked in ½ cup hot water
2 cups coconut milk made from 50 gm (⅔ cup) fresh grated coconut

Dry roast and grind to a fine paste:
12 almonds
10 cashew nuts
2 tsp sesame seeds (til)
1 tbsp ground nuts
1 tbsp roasted gram (bhuné chané)
5 tbsp dry grated coconut
3 tbsp coriander seeds
2 tsp cumin seeds
10 dried red chillies

Garnish:

Sprigs of mint leaves

- Heat oil in a non-stick pan.

- Fry cloves, cinnamon, peppercorns and 5 curry leaves for one minute.

- Add potatoes and fry for 6-7 minutes. Remove spices and potatoes from pan, drain and keep aside.

- Add onions, garlic and ginger to pan and fry till golden.

- Add chicken and fry for 8-9 minutes, stirring constantly.

- Stir in turmeric, garam masala, salt, remaining curry leaves and one cup water.

- Transfer to a deep pan. Cover pan and simmer for 15 minutes.

- Add ground masala paste and stir.

- Squeeze tamarind and strain in juice. Simmer for a further 5 minutes.

- Add coconut milk and fried potatoes and whole spices, and cook for about 10 minutes more, till chicken is tender and gravy is thick.

- Place chicken in a dish and garnish with sprigs of mint leaves.

- Serve with plain boiled rice.

MURGHI NA FARCHA

Fried Chicken – Parsi Style

Serves: 4

1 kg chicken legs
1 tsp salt
4-5 tbsp breadcrumbs
2 eggs, well beaten
Oil for deep frying

Grind to a fine paste:
3 dry red Kashmiri chillies, deseeded
8 cloves of garlic
1½ tsp ginger, grated
1 tsp cumin seeds
½ tsp coriander seeds

- Cut each chicken leg into 2 pieces at the joint. Wash chicken and dry with paper napkins.

- Make deep cuts in the flesh. Add salt to ground paste and rub onto chicken.

- Marinate chicken for 3 hours.

- Put chicken with one cup water in a pan. Cover pan and cook over low heat till chicken is three-quarters done. Drain chicken and allow to cool.

- Heat oil for deep frying in a kadahi or wok.

- Coat chicken with breadcrumbs, dip into beaten eggs and fry till light brown.

- Serve with French fries and sautéd vegetables.

SALI MA MURGHI

Chicken with Straw Potatoes

Serves: 4

1 kg chicken legs
1 tsp ground garlic
1 tsp ground ginger
3 tbsp oil
4 large onions, sliced
2 pieces cinnamon, 1" each
2 bay leaves
1½ tsp chilli powder
1 tsp salt

Garnish:

Straw potatoes (sali)

- Cut chicken legs into two pieces at the joint and make deep cuts in the flesh.

- Apply garlic and ginger onto chicken and allow to marinate for 2 hours.

- Heat oil in a non-stick pan and fry onions till golden.

- Add cinnamon and bay leaves and fry for a few seconds.

- Add chilli powder, salt and chicken and fry for 8 minutes, stirring constantly.

- Stir in one cup water, cover pan and simmer till chicken is tender.

- Place chicken in a dish and garnish with straw potatoes.

- Serve with roti.

Note: Three-quarter teaspoon sugar may be added with chilli powder if desired.

Straw potatoes are readily available with most grocers.

KAJU MA MURGHI

Chicken with Cashew Nuts

Serves: 4

1 kg chicken legs
1 tsp ground garlic
1 tsp ground ginger
1 tsp salt
4 tbsp oil
1 onion, sliced

Grind to a smooth paste:
1 tsp cumin seeds
1 cup chopped coriander leaves
5 green chillies
100 gm (¾ cup) broken cashew nuts
½ tsp salt

Garnish:
4 medium-sized potatoes, boiled, diced and lightly fried

- Cut each leg into two pieces at the joint. Make deep cuts in each piece.

- Apply garlic, ginger and salt on chicken and allow to marinate for half an hour.

- Heat 2 tablespoons oil in a non-stick pan and fry onions over medium heat till golden.

- Add chicken and fry for 8-9 minutes, stirring constantly.

- Stir in one cup water, cover pan and cook over low heat till chicken is three-quarters done.

- Heat 2 tablespoons oil in another pan and fry cashew nut paste for 7-8 minutes, stirring constantly to ensure that the cashew nut does not stick to pan and burn.

- Add chicken and three-quarter cup water and simmer on low heat for 5-6 minutes till gravy is thick.

- Garnish with boiled, quartered, fried potatoes.

Note: The dish can be made into a curry by adding 1 cup coconut milk, made from half a grated coconut, to the fried cashew nut paste, along with the chicken.

MURGHI NU DHANSAKH

Chicken with Lentils and Vegetables

Serves: 6

Dhan sakh is one of the best known of Parsi dishes. Its origin is probably the Iranian dish khoreste esfannaj, which is made with meat, lentils and spinach.

It is a favourite Sunday lunch in most Parsi homes.

1 kg chicken, jointed
2 tbsp dhansakh masala powder or 1 tbsp each powdered, roasted cumin seeds and coriander seeds
1 tsp sambhaar masala (optional)
3 tbsp oil
1 onion, chopped
A marble sized piece of tamarind soaked in ½ cup hot water

Dal:

1 cup pigeon peas (toover or arhar dal)
¼ tsp turmeric powder
3 spring onions with stems
1 medium-sized tomato
1 small aubergine (baigan)
150 gm red pumpkin (kuddu)
1 small potato
2 tbsp chopped fenugreek leaves (methi) or 1 tsp dry fenugreek leaves (kasuri methi)
2 tsp salt

Grind to a smooth paste:

8 cloves garlic
2" piece ginger
6-7 black peppercorns
6-7 cloves
6-7 green cardamoms
2 pieces cinnamon, 1" each
2 dry red Kashmiri chillies
¾ cup chopped mint leaves
½ cup chopped coriander leaves
5-6 green chillies
1 tbsp cumin seeds

- Wash dal and soak in water for 8-10 hours.

- Pressure cook dal along with remaining ingredients for dal with 5 cups water for 10 minute. Cool and remove pressure.

- Blend with a beater, or purée in a liquidizer or food processor.

- Place puréed dal mixture with chicken, dhan sakh and sambhaar masala in a pan.

- Cover pan and simmer till chicken is three-quarters cooked, stirring occasionally.

- Heat oil in another pan and fry chopped onion till golden.

- Add ground masala paste and fry till oil starts to bubble on top.

- Mix in chicken and dal mixture.

- Squeeze tamarind and strain in juice.

- Cover pan and simmer for 15 minutes.

- Serve with brown rice and kachumber

Note: Sambhaar masala used by the Parsis is quite different from the South Indian sambar masala.

Dhan sakh and sambhaar masala are available in specialized shops, selling spices.

ALETI PALETI

Savoury Chicken Liver and Gizzard

Serves: 4

This dish is served at Parsi weddings to the family members who sit down to eat after all the guests have departed.

½ kg chicken liver, cut into halves
½ kg chicken gizzard, cut into halves
4-5 tbsp oil
400 gm (6 medium-sized) onions, sliced
3 bay leaves
¾ tsp chilli powder
½ tsp turmeric powder
½ tsp coriander seeds, roasted and ground
½ tsp cumin seeds, roasted and ground
1 large tomato, thinly sliced
1½ tsp salt

Grind to a fine paste:
10 dry red Kashmiri chillies, deseeded
6 green chillies
¾ cup chopped coriander leaves
8 cloves of garlic
3" piece ginger
1½ tsp cumin seeds.

- Heat oil in a non-stick pan.

- Add onions and bay leaves and fry till onions are brown.

- Stir in ground masala, liver and gizzard. Fry over

low heat tossing and turning ingredients for 7-8 minutes.

- Add remaining ingredients and stir well. Cover pan and simmer for 10-15 minutes, stirring frequently till gizzards are done.

- Serve with bread.

KALA MASALA KAJU MURGH

Chicken with Cashew Nuts and Black Pepper – Maharashtra Style

Serves: 2

½ kg chicken, cut into 8 pieces
¼ kg (1¾ cups) cashew nuts
½ grated coconut
12 cloves garlic
1½" piece fresh ginger
2½ tbsp coriander seeds
1½ tsp cumin seeds
4 dried red chillies
6 cloves
3 pieces cinnamon, 1" each
2 tsp poppy seeds (khus khus)
1 tsp caraway seeds (shahi jeera)
½ tsp sesame seeds (til)
1 large onion, chopped
½ tsp black peppercorn, coarsely ground
4 tbsp oil
1½ tsp salt

- Grind about 20 cashew nuts with a little water and keep aside.

- Heat a tava, griddle or pan. Reduce heat to very low and add coconut and next 10 ingredients. Roast for 5 minutes, stirring continuously.

- Add onion and 50 gm (⅓ cup) cashew nuts and continue roasting for a further ten minutes.

- Remove from heat and cool.

- Add pepper powder and grind with three-quarter cup water to a smooth paste.

- Heat oil in a pan. Add ground spices and fry for ten minutes on low heat, stirring continuously.

- Add ground cashew nut paste, 5-6 whole cashew nuts and salt. Fry for 2-3 minutes further.

- Add chicken and fry for 5 minutes on high heat, stirring constantly.

- Add 3 cups water, reduce heat, cover pan and cook for 10 minutes.

- Add remaining whole cashew nuts and continue cooking till chicken is tender and curry is thick.

- Serve with plain boiled rice.

PANDHRA RASSA

Chicken Curry – Kolhapur Style

Serves: 6

1 kg chicken, jointed
1 fresh coconut, grated
4 tbsp oil
2 dry red chillies
3-4 cloves
3 pieces of cinnamon 1" each
2 tbsp cashew nuts
2 tbsp sultanas (kishmish)
1½ tsp salt
2 onions, grated
¾ cup curd, beaten till smooth

Marinade:

1½ tsp ground garlic
1½ tsp ground ginger

Grind to a smooth paste:

1 tsp caraway seeds (shahi jeera)
1½ tsp chilli powder
2 tsp coriander seeds
2 tsp poppy seeds (khus khus)
6-7 cloves
6-7 green cardamoms
4 tbsp desiccated coconut

- Mix ingredients for marinade and apply to chicken. Allow to marinate for 15 minutes.

- Blend fresh coconut with 2 cups water. Strain

coconut milk and keep aside.

- Heat 2 tablespoons oil in a non-stick pan and fry chicken till golden.

- Add in dry red chillies, cloves, cinnamon, cashew nuts and sultanas. Fry for 2-3 minutes.

- Transfer to a deep pan and add one cup water and salt. Cover pan and cook on low heat till chicken is tender.

- Heat remaining oil in a non-stick pan and fry onions till golden.

- Add ground masala paste and fry for 5 minutes.

- Mix in curd and simmer for 2-3 minutes.

- Add to chicken and cook further for 5-6 minutes.

- Add coconut milk and continue cooking, stirring continuously, till it comes to boil.

- Remove pan immediately from heat.

- Serve with plain boiled rice.

PATHARÉ PRABHU KOMBRI MASALA

Chicken Patharé Prabhu

Serves: 2

Patharé Prabhu is the name of a Maharashtrian community living in Mumbai. This is one of their famous chicken dishes.

½ kg chicken, jointed

Dry roast and grind:

1 tsp coriander seeds
½ Bengal gram (chané ki dal)
½ tsp whole wheat
½ tsp mustard seeds
½ tsp cumin seeds

Marinade:

½ tsp turmeric powder
½ tsp chilli powder
1 tsp ground garlic
1 tsp ground ginger

Gravy:

3 tbsp oil
¼ tsp asafoetida (hing)
1 onion, grated
1 tsp salt

- Mix ingredients for marinade with ground masala.

Rub into chicken and leave for one hour.

- Heat oil for gravy in a pan and add asafoetida. Fry for a moment and add onion. Fry till onion is light brown.

- Add marinated chicken, salt and 2 cups water. Simmer on medium heat for 25 minutes, till chicken is tender.

- Serve with plain boiled rice or roti.

Note: The ground masala used in this recipe is a traditional Patharé Prabhu masala.

GOAN KOMBI MASALA

Chicken Curry – Goa Style

Serves: 6

1 kg boneless chicken, cut into 3" cubes
1½ tsp salt
¼ tsp turmeric powder
4 tbsp oil
4 onions, sliced-
50 gm tamarind, soaked in 1 cup hot water

Grind to a smooth paste:
60 gm dried red chillies
1 tbsp ground garlic
1 tbsp ground ginger
1 tbsp cumin seeds
8-9 green cardamoms
3 pieces cinnamon, 1" each
½ cup Goa palm vinegar or malt vinegar

- Rub chicken with salt and turmeric powder. Marinate for 15 minutes.

- Heat oil in a non-stick pan and fry chicken till well browned. Remove from pan, drain and keep aside.

- Add onions to pan and fry till brown.

- Add ground paste and fry for 5 minutes

- Mix in chicken and 3 cups water.

- Squeeze tamarind, strain juice into curry and stir well.

- Cover pan and cook on low heat till chicken is tender.
- Serve with plain boiled rice.

XACUTI

Thick Chicken Curry – Goa Style

Serves: 6

1½ kg chicken, jointed
1 coconut, grated
250 gm (2 large) onions, chopped
1+4 tbsp oil
½ tsp turmeric powder
1½ tsp salt
¼ tsp powdered nutmeg
¼ tsp powdered mace (javitri)
2 tbsp tamarind, soaked in ½ cup hot water

Masala for grinding:
20 Kashmiri red chillies
15 cloves garlic
3 pieces cinnamon, 1" each
8-10 cloves
10 black peppercorns
2 tsp coriander seeds
½ tbsp cumin seeds
1 tbsp poppy seeds (khus khus)

- Heat a tava or griddle and gently roast grated coconut for 4-5 minutes.

- Remove coconut and roast half the onions for 5-6 minutes. Keep aside.

- Heat one tablespoon oil in a non-stick frying pan and lightly fry ingredients for masala.

Main Course Dishes   **169**

- Cool and grind with roasted coconut and onion to a fine paste.

- Heat 4 tablespoons oil in a pan and fry remaining onions till brown.

- Add chicken and fry for 8 minutes till golden, turning frequently.

- Add ground spices and turmeric, mix well and fry for 5 minutes.

- Mix in 2 cups water, salt, nutmeg and mace. Cover pan and cook on low heat for 15 minutes.

- Squeeze tamarind and strain juice into chicken. Cook till chicken is tender.

- Serve with plain boiled rice, bread or roti.

KODI TAMATAR

Chicken with tomatoes – Andhra Style

Serves: 4

1 kg chicken, jointed
4 tbsp oil
4 onions, chopped
6-7 curry leaves
1 tsp ground garlic
1 tsp ground ginger
3 tsp chilli powder
½ tsp turmeric powder
2 tbsp coriander powder
1 tsp cumin powder
4 tomatoes, chopped
1 tsp tamarind pulp
1 tsp salt
3 green chillies, chopped

- Heat oil in a kadahi or wok and add onions and curry leaves. Fry till onions are translucent. Mix in ginger, garlic and powdered spices, and fry till brown.

- Add chicken and continue to fry till brown, stirring frequently.

- Add tomatoes, tamarind pulp, salt and 1½ cups water. Cover pan and simmer till chicken is tender.

- Stir in green chillies.

- Serve with rice.

KORIGASHI

Chicken Curry with Coconut – Mangalore Style

Serves: 4

1 kg boneless chicken, cut into 3" cubes
2 cups grated coconut
5-6 tbsp oil
10-12 dried red chillies
5-6 black peppercorns
3-4 cloves
1" piece cinnamon
2 cups grated onions
1 tbsp ground garlic
1 tbsp ground ginger
3 tbsp coriander seeds
1 tsp cumin seeds
½ tsp fenugreek seeds
1 tsp mustard seeds
1 tsp tamarind pulp
1½ tsp salt
10 curry leaves

- Soak one cup grated coconut in 4 cups hot water for ten minutes. Blend well in a liquidizer or food processor and strain coconut milk.

- Heat one tablespoon oil in a non-stick pan and fry remaining grated coconut for 5-6 minutes, till golden. Keep aside.

- Heat one tablespoon oil in a another non-stick pan and lightly fry red chillies.

- Add whole spices and fry for 2 minutes, stirring constantly.

- Grind together, fried coconut and whole spices, one cup onions and next 7 ingredients with half cup coconut milk.

- Heat 3 tablespoons oil in a non-stick pan and fry remaining onions till golden brown.

- Stir in spice paste and fry for about 5 minutes, till oil starts to bubble on top.

- Add chicken, salt and curry leaves, and continue frying for 8-9 minutes, stirring frequently.

- Add remaining coconut milk, cover pan and cook on low heat till chicken is tender.

- The gravy should have a thin flowing consistency. Add extra water if necessary.

- Serve with plain boiled rice.

NARAL CHI KOMBRI – 1

Chicken Curry – Konkan Style

Serves: 2

½ kg chicken, jointed
3 tbsp oil
3-4 green cardamoms
3-4 pieces cinnamon, 1" each
3-4 cloves
2 onions, grated
1 tsp ground garlic
1 tsp ground ginger
1 tsp Kashmiri chilli powder (optional)
1 tsp salt
1-2 cups chopped tomatoes
3 tsp Konkani masala
1 cup chopped coriander leaves
1 cup coconut milk, extracted from ¾ cup grated coconut

- Heat oil in a non-stick pan and fry whole spices for one minute.

- Add onion, garlic and ginger and fry till brown.

- Add chilli powder and salt, stir for a moment and add tomatoes. Fry till oil starts to bubble on top.

- Mix in one cup water. Bring to boil and add chicken and coriander leaves. Cover pan and cook on low heat till tender.

- Add coconut milk and continue cooking on low heat for a minute longer.

NARAL CHI KOMBRI – 2

Chicken Curry – Konkan Style

Serves: 2

½ kg chicken, jointed

Marinade:

3 tsp Konkani masala
½ tsp turmeric powder
½ tsp chilli powder
1 tsp ground garlic
1 tsp ground ginger

Gravy:

3 tbsp oil
¼ tsp asafoetida (hing)
1 onion, grated
1 tsp salt

- Mix ingredients for marinade and rub into chicken. Allow to marinate for one hour.

- Heat oil in a pan. Add asafoetida and onion and fry till onion is light brown.

- Add in marinated chicken, salt and 2 cups water. Cover pan and cook for 25 minutes, till chicken is tender.

- Serve with plain boiled rice.

KOMBRI CHA SALNA

Chicken in Crab Masala – Konkan Style

Serves: 2

½ kg boneless chicken, cut into 2" cubes
1 onion, chopped
1 cup curd, beaten till smooth
2 tsp Konkani masala
1 tsp salt
1 tbsp tamarind soaked in ½ cup hot water

Dry roast individually and grind in 1 cup water:
1 onion
1 cup grated fresh coconut
1 tsp cumin seeds
1 tsp coriander seeds
4-5 cloves
4-5 pieces cinnamon, 1" each
4-5 green cardamoms
10 whole black peppercorns
10 cloves garlic

Garnish:

Chopped coriander leaves

- Heat oil in a pan and fry onion till brown.
- Add ground masala and fry till light brown.
- Mix in chicken and fry for 7-8 minutes, turning chicken frequently.
- Add Konkani masala and salt, stir and add one cup

water. Squeeze tamarind and strain in juice.

- Cover pan and cook on low heat till chicken is tender.

- Add curd and cook for 6-7 minutes.

- Place chicken in a dish and garnish with coriander leaves.

- Serve with plain boiled rice or roti.

KAIREE CHI KOMBRI

Chicken Curry – Konkan Style

Serves: 2

½ kg chicken, jointed
1 cup grated coconut
1 onion, sliced
½ cup chopped tomatoes
1 tsp ground garlic
1 tsp salt
2 tbsp oil
4 tsp Konkani masala
1 raw mango or ⅓ cup dry mango, diced

Garnish:

1 tbsp chopped coriander leaves

- Blend grated coconut with one cup warm water. Strain milk and keep aside.

- Mix onion, tomatoes, garlic, salt and oil in a pan, with your hand, crushing it to a thick paste.

- Add chicken, place pan on heat and fry for 7-8 minutes, turning frequently.

- Mix in Konkani masala, mango and 3 cups water. Bring to boil, reduce heat and cook till chicken is tender.

- Add coconut milk and cook on low heat for one minute.

- Place chicken curry in a dish and garnish with

coriander leaves.

- Serve with plain boiled rice.

Note: The curry should not be boiled after the coconut milk has been added.

KOZHI KUZHUMBU

Chicken Curry – Madras Style

Serves: 4

750 gm chicken, jointed
4 tbsp oil
1 tsp mustard seeds
15 curry leaves
3 medium-sized onions, chopped
1½ tsp chilli powder
¼ tsp turmeric powder
2 tbsp poppy seeds (khus khus), ground
2 tbsp tamarind, without seeds or strings, soaked in 1 cup hot water
1 tsp salt
1 tsp fenugreek seeds (methi), ground
1 tsp cumin seeds, ground

Marinade:

2 tbsp lime juice
½ tsp salt

Grind to a fine paste:

2 medium-sized coconuts, grated
1½ tsp chopped garlic
1½ tsp chopped ginger
400 gm (8 medium-sized) tomatoes, chopped

Garnish:

Chopped coriander leaves

- Mix ingredients for marinade and rub into chicken.
  Allow to marinate for 10 minutes.

- Heat oil in a non-stick pan and add mustard seeds. Allow to splutter and add curry leaves and onions. Fry till onions are brown.

- Stir in chilli powder and turmeric powder.

- Mix poppy seeds with ground coconut paste and add to pan. Fry for 8-9 minutes.

- Add chicken and fry for 8 minutes, stirring frequently.

- Squeeze tamarind and strain juice into pan with 2 cups water, salt, fenugreek seeds and cumin seeds.

- Cover pan and cook on low heat till chicken is tender.

- Place chicken in a dish and garnish with chopped coriander leaves.

- Serve with plain boiled rice.

KOZHI VARATHA KOSAMBU

Chicken Chettinad

Serves: 6

1 kg chicken, jointed
3 tbsp oil
2 tsp ground garlic
2 tsp ground ginger
1 onion, grated
1½ tsp salt
2 tsp garam masala powder
2 tsp chilli powder
½ tsp turmeric powder
3 tsp powdered aniseed (saunf)
1½ tbsp powdered poppy seeds (khus khus)
½ coconut, ground
1 star anise (badian)
6-7 powdered green cardamoms
5-6 curry leaves
1 cup fresh tomato purée made from 3 large tomatoes

Garnish:

Chopped coriander leaves

- Heat oil in a non-stick pan.

- Fry garlic, ginger and onions till light brown.

- Add all powdered spices and coconut paste. Fry for 5 minutes.

- Add chicken, star anise, cardamom and curry leaves.

- Fry for 8-9 minutes, stirring frequently.

- Stir in tomato purée and continue cooking on medium heat till oil starts to bubble on top.

- Add 2 cups water. Cover pan and cook on low heat till chicken is tender.

- Place chicken in a dish and garnish with chopped coriander leaves.

KOZHI CHETTINAD

Chicken Fry – Chettinad Style

Serves: 4

1 kg chicken, cut into 8 pieces
3 tbsp oil
2 cloves
5-6 black peppercorns
1" piece cinnamon
1 tsp aniseed (saunf)
1 tsp cumin seeds
6-8 curry leaves

Marinade:

2 onions, chopped
1 tsp ground ginger
1 tsp ground garlic
20 dry red chillies
1 tbsp lime juice
1 tsp salt
¼ tsp turmeric powder

- Grind ingredients for marinade to a fine paste.

- Make deep cuts in chicken flesh.

- Apply marinade onto chicken and allow to marinate for 3 hours.

- Heat oil in a non-stick pan and add all spices, except curry leaves and sauté for one minute.

- Add curry leaves and chicken and fry for 2-3 minutes.

- Reduce heat, cover pan and cook, turning chicken frequently till tender.
- Sprinkle about one-third cup water over chicken, if necessary.

KOZHI ERACHI PAAL CURRY

Chicken in Coconut Curry – Kerela Style

Serves: 2

½ kg chicken, jointed
2 cups grated coconut
3 tbsp oil
1 tsp mustard seeds
1 onion, sliced
1 tsp garlic,chopped
1 tsp ginger, chopped
8-10 curry leaves
2 tbsp coriander powder
1½ tsp chilli powder
½ tsp turmeric powder
1 tsp salt
1 tbsp vinegar

Garnish:

Dried red chillies (optional)
Lime slices (optional)

- Blend coconut with half cup warm water in a liquidizer or food processor. Strain thick coconut milk and keep aside.

- Blend strained coconut again, with 2 cups warm water. Strain thin coconut milk and keep aside.

- Heat oil in a pan and add mustard seeds. Allow to splutter and add onions. Fry for 2-3 minutes till golden.

- Add ginger, garlic and curry leaves and fry for a further 2 minutes.

- Mix in powdered spices. Fry for one minute.

- Add chicken, salt and vinegar and fry for 5 minutes.

- Add 2 cups thin coconut milk.

- Cover pan and cook over low heat till chicken is tender.

- Stir in half cup thick coconut milk.

- Bring to boil and remove from heat immediately.

- Garnish with red chillies and slices of lime.

- Serve with plain boiled rice.

KOZHI CURRY

Chicken Curry – Malabar Style

Serves: 4

1 kg chicken, jointed
4 tbsp oil
2 onions, sliced
10 black peppercorns
2 tsp ground garlic
2 tsp ground ginger
½ tsp turmeric powder
3 tomatoes, chopped
2 tsp powdered poppy seeds (khus khus)
2 tsp ground sultanas (kishmish)
1½ tbsp chilli powder
1½ tsp coriander powder
1½ tsp salt
4 tbsp curd, beaten till smooth
1 tsp lime juice
A pinch of sugar

- Heat oil in a pan and fry onions till brown. Add peppercorns, garlic, ginger and turmeric powder. Fry for a minute.

- Add tomatoes, and continue frying till oil starts to bubble on top.

- Add poppy seeds, sultanas, chilli powder, coriander powder and salt and fry for one minute.

- Add chicken, and fry for 7-8 minutes stirring constantly.

- Add 3 cups water. Cover pan and cook till chicken is tender.
- Stir in beaten curd, lime juice and sugar and cook further for 5 minutes.

KOZHI VARATTIYATHU

Chicken Masala – Malabar Style

Serves: 2

½ kg chicken, cut into 3 " pieces
2 tbsp coconut oil
1 tsp mustard seeds
2 dried red chillies
20 curry leaves
1 tsp salt
1 tsp chilli powder

Dry roast individually and grind to a fine paste:
1 star anise (badiyan)
2 pieces cinnamon, 1 " each
3-4 cloves
3-4 whole green cardamoms
1 tbsp poppy seeds (khus khus)
3 tbsp coriander seeds
½ cup grated fresh coconut

Garnish:
Freshly ground black pepper

- Heat oil in a pan and add mustard seeds, dried red chillies and 10 curry leaves. Fry for a few moments.

- Add chicken and fry for a minute.

- Mix in ground paste and continue frying for 1-2 minutes more.

- Add 1½ cups water, salt, chilli powder and

remaining 10 curry leaves.

- Cover pan and cook over low heat till chicken is tender.

- Place chicken in a dish and sprinkle over, a little freshly ground black pepper.

KOZHI ISTU

Chicken and Vegetable Curry – Kerala Style

Serves: 4

½ kg boneless chicken, cut into 3" cubes
2 cups grated coconut
3 tbsp oil
1" piece cinnamon
3-4 black peppercorns
3-4 green cardamoms
3-4 cloves
3 onions, grated
1 tsp ground ginger
1 tbsp chopped green chillies
2 bay leaves
A pinch of turmeric powder (optional)
½ tsp powdered aniseed (saunf)
1 tsp salt
5 potatoes, quartered
1 carrot, sliced
½ cup shelled green peas
8-10 curry leaves
4-5 cloves garlic, sliced
1 tbsp sliced ginger

- Blend coconut with 3 cups hot water in a liquidizer or food processor. Strain coconut milk and keep aside.

- Heat oil in a non-stick pan and fry cinnamon, peppercorns, cardamom and cloves for a few moments.

- Add onions, ground ginger, and green chillies and fry for ten minutes.

- Mix in chicken, bay leaves, turmeric powder, aniseed and salt. Fry for 8-9 minutes.

- Transfer chicken to a deep pan and add 3 cups water.

- Cover pan and cook for 10 minutes.

- Add vegetables, curry leaves, sliced garlic and ginger. Cook till vegetables are tender.

- Serve with rice.

Rice

Rice is a symbol of fertility and prosperity and is considered auspicious by most communities. It is the staple food of the coastal regions and southern and hilly areas of India. Basmati rice is the most popular for its special flavour and long grain. It is especially used in the preparation of biryani and pulao.

The word pulao appears both in Sanskrit and Tamil literature. It is also ascribed to the Persian and Arabic *pilav*. Pulao is a combination of rice and spiced cooked meat, while biryani is a combination of spicy, saffron flavoured meat, layered with rice.

Favourite accompaniments with biryani and pulao are kachumber, pickled onions, plain curd and raita—spiced curd.

MURGH PULAO

Chicken Pulao

Serves: 4

Chicken:

¾ kg boneless chicken, cut into 3" cubes
1 tsp ground garlic,
1 tsp ground ginger
1 tsp ground whole green cardamom
2 pieces cinnamon, 1" each
2 bay leaves (tej patta)
1 tsp salt

Rice:

2 cups basmati rice
3-4 tbsp oil
½ tsp garam masala powder
1 tsp salt

Garnish:

1 onion, sliced

- Place all ingredients for chicken in a pan with 5 cups water. Cover pan and cook on low heat for 10 minutes.

- Wash rice and soak in plenty of water for half an hour. Drain.

- Heat oil for rice in a non-stick pan. Add onion for garnish and fry till golden brown. Remove onion from pan, drain and keep aside. Add rice to pan and fry for 6-7 minutes, stirring continuously.

- Add chicken with 4½ cups stock, garam masala powder and salt.

- Stir gently, cover pan and cook on low heat till rice is tender and dry.

- Place pulao on a platter and garnish with reserved fried onions.

GOAN KOMBI PULAO

Chicken Pulao – Goa Style

Serves: 4

400 gm boneless chicken, cut into 3" cubes
1½ tsp salt
250 gm (1¼ cups) rice
3 tbsp oil
3-4 pieces cinnamon, 1" each
3-4 green cardamoms
3-4 cloves
2 onions, grated
1 tsp ground garlic
1 tsp ground ginger
3 tomatoes, chopped

Garnish:

100 gm cooked ham, cubed

- Place chicken, salt and 4 cups water in a pan and cook on low heat for 15 minutes.

- Wash rice and soak in water for half an hour. Drain.

- Heat oil in a pan and add next six ingredients. Fry till onions are brown.

- Add rice and continue frying for 8-9 minutes.

- Stir in tomatoes and cook for 7-8 minutes.

- Add chicken with 3 cups stock. Cover pan and cook on low heat till rice is tender and dry.

- Place pulao in a platter and garnish with ham cubes.

KOMRI PULAO

Chicken and Coconut Pulao – Konkan Style

Serves: 3-4

½ kg boneless chicken, cut into 3" cubes
½ fresh coconut, grated
2 tbsp oil
1 tsp ground garlic
1 tsp ground ginger
2 onions, grated
1 tsp chilli powder
1 tsp Konkani masala
1 tsp salt
1 cup kolum or basmati rice
1 cup tomato purée, made from 3 large tomatoes

- Blend coconut in a liquidizer or food processor with one cup warm water. Strain thick coconut milk and use for any other purpose.

- Blend strained coconut again with one cup warm water. Strain thin coconut milk and reserve.

- Heat oil in a non-stick pan and fry garlic, ginger and onion till brown.

- Add chicken, powdered spices and salt and fry for 8 minutes, stirring constantly.

- Add tomato purée and continue frying till oil starts to bubble on top.

- Transfer chicken to a deep pan and add 3 cups water.

- Cover pan and simmer till chicken is tender. There should be one cup gravy left in the pan.

- Wash rice and soak in water for 15 minutes.

- Drain rice and add to chicken with one cup reserved thin coconut milk.

- Stir gently, cover pan and cook on low heat till rice is tender.

GOLYACHA MURGH PULAO

Chicken Meatball Pulao

Serves: 6

Meatballs:

¾ kg chicken
½ cup Bengal gram (chané ki dal), soaked for 1 hour
1 tsp ground garlic
1 tsp ground ginger
1 tsp powdered coriander seeds
1 tsp powdered cumin seeds
1 tsp chilli powder
1 tsp salt
¼ tsp turmeric powder
1 tbsp whole wheat flour (atta)

Masala for meatballs:

1 cup grated coconut
1 tsp ground garlic
1 tsp ground ginger
1 tsp chilli powder
1 tbsp powdered caraway seeds (shahi jeera)
4-5 cloves, powdered
1" piece cinnamon, powdered
2 tbsp oil

Rice:

½ kg (2½ cups) basmati or jirga rice
4 tbsp oil
2 onions, sliced
⅓ cup cashew nuts
⅓ cup sultanas (kishmish)
3 cloves

4 cardamoms
2 bay leaves (tej patta)
1 tsp salt
¼ tsp saffron soaked in 1 tsp rose-water

- Debone chicken and mince meat.

- Mix mince with remaining ingredients for meatballs and grind mixture to a smooth paste.

- Shape into small balls and steam for 12-15 minutes.

- Cook chicken bones with 6 cups water in a pressure cooker for 20 minutes. Strain stock.

- Wash rice and soak in water for half an hour. Drain.

- Mix all ingredients for masala, except oil.

- Heat oil for masala in a non-stick pan. Add masala and fry till oil starts to bubble on top.

- Add meat balls and fry for 5 minutes, stirring gently.

- Heat 4 tablespoons oil for rice in another pan and fry onions till brown and crisp. Remove onions from pan and drain.

- Add cashew nuts and sultanas and fry till cashew nuts are golden. Remove from pan and drain.

- Add cloves, cardamom and bay leaves to pan and fry for a few moments.

- Add rice and continue frying for 8-9 minutes, stirring constantly.

- Stir in salt and 4½ cups stock.

- Cover pan and cook on low heat till rice is cooked.

- Place one-third of the rice in a deep pan. Place half the meatballs over the rice. Sprinkle over one-third onions. Cover with another one-third rice. Place remaining meatballs over rice, sprinkle with one-third onions and cover with remaining rice. Sprinkle with cashew nuts, sultanas, remaining onions and saffron.

- Cover pan and cook on very low heat for 5-7 minutes.

- Serve with Kolhapuri chutney and papad.

MURGH TIKKA PULAO

Barbecued Chicken Pulao

Serves: 4

The aromatic flavour of saffron pulao and spicy tender chicken takes you back to the days of the Moghuls and Nawabs.

You will need skewers to prepare this dish.

½ kg boneless chicken, cut into 2½" cubes
1 tbsp cream
A pinch of powdered saffron

Marinade:

1 onion, sliced
1 tsp ground garlic
2 tbsp lime juice
1 tsp salt
½ tsp freshly ground black pepper
1 tbsp oil

Rice:

2 cups basmati rice
1 tsp salt
2-3 tbsp butter
2 egg yolks, beaten
¼ tsp black pepper

Garnish:

¼ tsp whole black peppercorn
Cherry tomatoes

- Mix ingredients for marinade with chicken and marinate for 2-4 hours.

- Mix saffron with cream.

- String chicken pieces onto a skewer. Brush with saffron and cream mixture.

- Wash rice and soak in water for one hour.

- Cook rice in plenty of boiling water with salt, till tender. Drain.

- Mix butter and beaten egg yolk into rice gently with a fork. Place rice on low heat and cook for 4-5 minutes.

- Grill chicken over a charcoal fire, regular clay or gas tandoor, or electric grill for 8-9 minutes, basting with saffron and cream mixture.

- Place rice on a platter. Arrange chicken with skewers on top of rice.

- Scatter peppercorn and cherry tomatoes around and serve.

DUMPUKHT MURGH BIRYANI

Chicken Biryani

Serves: 4

¾ kg chicken, jointed
3 tbsp oil
1 tsp ground garlic
1 tsp ground ginger
3 medium-sized onions, grated
1 tbsp ground cashew nuts
1 tbsp powdered poppy seeds (khus khus)
1 tbsp ground dry coconut
1 cup fresh tomato purée made from 3 large tomatoes
2 cups basmati rice
1 tsp salt
¼ tsp saffron soaked in ⅓ cup milk
1 tbsp ghee for sprinkling on rice

Marinade:

2 cups thick curd, beaten till smooth
1 tbsp chopped green chillies
1 tbsp chopped coriander leaves
1½ tsp salt
1½ tsp chilli powder
1 tsp garam masala powder
½ tsp turmeric powder

- Mix ingredients for marinade to a smooth paste. Add chicken and marinate for 15 minutes.

- Heat oil in a non-stick pan and fry garlic, ginger and onion till light brown.

- Add cashew nuts, poppy seeds and coconut and fry for 2 minutes, stirring continuously.

- Stir in tomato purée and simmer on low heat till oil starts to bubble on top.

- Transfer fried paste to a deep large pan.

- Add chicken with marinade.

- Cover pan and cook on low heat till chicken is tender.

- Wash rice and soak for 15 minutes.

- Cook rice with salt in plenty of water till three-quarters done.

- Drain out water and allow rice to cool.

- Place one-third of the rice in a deep pan. Place half the chicken over the rice. Cover with another one-third rice. Place remaining chicken over rice and cover with remaining rice.

- Sprinkle saffron milk and ghee on top.

- Cover pan with lid and seal with a paste of flour and water.

- Place pan on a tava or griddle, place a few live coals on lid and cook on low heat for 45 minutes or bake in an oven at 180°C (350°C) for 25-30 minutes.

BIRYANI SHAHJEHANI

Chicken Biryani – Mughlai Style

Serves: 4

Chicken:

½ kg boneless chicken, cut into 3" cubes
4 tbsp oil
1 tsp ground garlic
1 tsp ground ginger
3 large onions, grated or ground
1 tbsp powdered poppy seeds (khus khus)
1 tbsp powdered cheronji (charoli)
1 tbsp ground cashew nuts
1 tbsp ground dry coconut
1 cup fresh tomato purée, made from 3 large tomatoes
1 tbsp lime juice

Marinade:

½ kg (2 cups) thick curd, beaten till smooth
1 tsp garam masala powder
2 tsp chilli powder
2 tsp salt
½ tsp turmeric powder
1 tbsp chopped coriander leaves
1 tbsp chopped green chillies
1 tbsp chopped mint leaves

Rice:

½ kg (2½ cups) basmati rice
1 tsp salt
¼ tsp saffron soaked in ⅓ cup warm milk
¼ tsp yellow or red food colouring
1 tbsp ghee

Chicken:

- Mix ingredients for marinade to a smooth paste.

- Rub marinade into chicken and allow to marinate for half an hour.

- Heat oil in a non-stick pan and lightly fry garlic and ginger.

- Add onions and fry till brown.

- Reduce heat and add poppy seeds, cheronji, cashew nuts and coconut. Fry for a few seconds.

- Stir in tomato purée and cook till masala is well fried and oil starts to bubble on top.

- Add chicken with marinade and lime juice.

- Cover pan and cook on low heat for 25 minutes, stirring occasionally till chicken is tender and gravy is thick.

Rice:

- Wash rice and soak in water for half an hour.

- Cook rice in plenty of water with salt till three-quarters done. Drain and allow rice to cool.

- Place one-third of the rice in a deep pan or oven-proof dish. Place half the chicken over the rice. Cover with another one-third rice. Place remaining chicken over rice and cover with remaining rice.

- Mix food colouring with saffron milk and sprinkle with ghee on top.

- Cook on dum or bake in an oven at 180°C (350°C)

for 30-40 minutes.

- Serve with curd and kachumber.

Note: Sultanas (kishmish), peeled and slivered almonds and grated coconut can be sprinkled on the rice before baking.

KACCHÉ MURGH KI BIRYANI

Chicken Biryani

Serves: 4

¾ kg chicken, jointed
400 gm (2 cups) basmati rice
4 tbsp ghee
3 large onions, finely sliced
1 tsp caraway seeds (shahi jeera)
1½ cups thick curd, beaten till smooth
1 cup fresh tomato purée, made from 3 large tomatoes
1½ tsp chilli powder
1½ tsp garam masala powder
½ tsp turmeric powder
1½ tsp salt
3 cardamoms
3 pieces cinnamon, 1" each
3 cloves
½ cup milk
½ tsp saffron
1 tbsp ghee for sprinkling on rice

Marinade:

1 tbsp ground garlic
1 tbsp ground ginger
1 tbsp ground coriander leaves
1 tbsp ground green chillies
1 tbsp lime juice

- Mix ingredients for marinade and rub into chicken. Allow to marinate for one hour.
- Wash rice and soak in water for one hour.

- Heat ghee in a non-stick pan and fry onions till brown. Remove onions from pan and drain. Grind half the onions.

- Remove pan from heat and add caraway seeds. Stir and pour contents of pan over chicken.

- Mix curd, tomato purée, powdered spices, salt and fried ground onions. Add chicken and mix well.

- Boil rice in plenty of water with cardamom, cinnamon and cloves till half done.

- Drain rice, reserving one cup water and whole spices.

- Mix saffron in hot milk and reserved rice water.

- Spread chicken mixture in a deep pan. Sprinkle in reserved fried onions and cover with rice mixed with reserved whole spices. Sprinkle saffron mixture and ghee over rice.

- Cook on dum or bake in an oven at 180° C (350°F) for 40 minutes.

BOHRI MURGH BIRYANI

Chicken Biryani – Bohra Style

Serves: 6

1 kg chicken, jointed
1 kg onions (8 large), sliced, fried crisp and drained
½ kg (3 large) potatoes, peeled and cut lengthwise into half
¾ kg (3¾ cups) rice
1 tbsp lime juice
4 tbsp oil
3 pieces cinnamon, 1" each
3 black cardamoms
6-7 black peppercorns
3 cloves
3 tsp caraway seeds
¼ tsp saffron soaked in ½ cup warm milk

Marinade:
½ kg tomatoes (3 large), blanched, peeled and chopped
½ kg (2 cups) curd, beaten till smooth
2 tsp ground garlic
2 tsp ground ginger
3 tsp cumin seeds
2 tsp garam masala powder
2-3 tsp chilli powder
½ tsp turmeric powder
2 tsp salt

- Mix ingredients for marinade well. Crush fried onions and add to marinade with potatoes and chicken. Mix well and allow to marinate for 4 hours.

- Wash rice and soak in plenty of water with lime juice for half an hour.

- Cook rice in soaking water till three-quarters done. Drain water.

- Heat oil in a deep pan. Lightly fry cinnamon, cardamom, cloves, peppercorns and caraway seeds.

- Arrange a thin layer of rice in a pan and place chicken, with marinade on top. Cover with remaining rice.

- Sprinkle saffron flavoured milk over rice.

- Cover pan and cook on very low heat for half an hour or bake in a preheated oven at 150° C (300° F) for half an hour, or cook on dum.

- Serve with plain beaten curd.

KOZHI BIRYANI

Chicken Biryani – Malabar Style

Serves: 5-6

¾ kg chicken, jointed
2 cups grated coconut
2 tbsp ghee
4-5 onions, sliced
¾ kg (3¾ cups) basmati rice
1 tbsp oil
1 tsp salt
⅓ cup warm milk
¼ tsp yellow food colour
½ cup ghee

Marinade:

2 tsp ground garlic
2 tsp ground ginger
3 cups curd, beaten till smooth
3 tbsp powdered dry coconut
3 tbsp powdered cashew nuts
3 tbsp chopped green chillies
1 cup chopped coriander leaves
½ cup chopped mint leaves
14 cloves
12 green cardamoms
3 pieces cinnamon, 1" each
1 tsp salt
1 tbsp lime juice

- Mix ingredients for marinade.

- Blend grated coconut with 1½ cups warm water in a

liquidiser or food processor. Strain coconut milk and add to marinade.

- Heat 2 tablespoons ghee in a pan and fry onions till brown and crisp.

- Remove onions from pan, drain and crush. Add to marinade.

- Add chicken to marinade and marinate for 2 hours.

- Pour any ghee remaining in the pan after frying onions, over chicken.

- Wash rice and cook in plenty of water with one tablespoon oil and one teaspoon salt, till half-cooked.

- Place chicken in a large pan and arrange rice over it.

- Mix milk with food colour and sprinkle over rice with half cup ghee.

- Cover pan and bake at 180°C (350°F) for 35-40 minutes.

Roti

KEEMA NAAN

Naan stuffed with Chicken Mince

Makes: 6

Dough:

½ kg flour (maida)
¼ tsp baking powder
½ tsp salt
1 cup warm milk
1 cup curd, beaten till smooth
¾ egg, lightly beaten
1 tsp ghee

Filling:

200 gm chicken mince
2 tbsp oil
½ tsp ground garlic
½ tsp ground ginger
¾ tsp chilli powder
½ tsp garam masala powder
¼ tsp turmeric powder
¾ tsp salt
¾ cup fresh tomato purée made from 2 large tomatoes
1 onion, chopped
1 tbsp chopped green chillies
1 tbsp chopped coriander leaves

Topping:

¼ egg
1 tbsp milk
1 tbsp onion seeds (kalaunji)
1 tbsp poppy seeds (khus khus)

- Mix all ingredients for dough and knead to a soft dough.

- Cover and leave aside for 3-4 hours.

- Heat oil for filling in a non-stick pan and lightly fry garlic and ginger.

- Add minced chicken and fry till pale gold, stirring continuously.

- Stir in powdered spices and salt, and fry for a few seconds.

- Add tomato purée and continue frying till oil starts to bubble on top.

- Remove from heat.

- Stir in onions, coriander leaves and green chillies.

- Allow filling to cool.

- Divide dough into 6 portions.

- Flatten one portion into a disc 3 inches in diameter. Place a portion of filling in the centre of the disc. Fold over dough to cover filling and pinch to seal. Shape into a flat round and roll out on a floured surface into a circle, 6 inches in diameter. Make remaining naan in the same way.

- Lightly beat egg and milk for topping and brush top of each naan with mixture. Sprinkle with poppy and onion seeds.

- Grill at 220° C (425°F) for 3-4 minutes. Turn over and grill for 2 minutes more. If your grill is not graded in degrees, then grill at maximum temperature for 3-4 minutes.

- Naan can be baked in a preheated oven at 220°C (425°F) for 3 minutes.

Note: Naan can be made without eggs, by omitting them while making the dough and adding a little extra curd to knead it.

KEEMA PARANTHA

Parantha Stuffed with Chicken Mince

Makes: 6

Dough:

½ kg (2 cups) whole wheat flour (atta)
1½ cups water

Filling:

200 gm chicken mince
2 tbsp oil
½ tsp ground garlic
½ tsp ground ginger
¾ tsp chilli powder
½ tsp garam masala powder
¼ tsp turmeric powder
¾ tsp salt
¾ cup fresh tomato purée made from 2 large tomatoes
1 onion, chopped
1 tbsp chopped green chillies
1 tbsp chopped coriander leaves

- Mix all ingredients for dough and knead to a soft dough.

- Cover and keep aside for one hour.

- Heat oil for filling in a non-stick pan and lightly fry garlic and ginger.

- Add minced chicken and fry till pale gold.

- Mix in powdered spices and salt.

- Add tomato purée and continue frying till oil starts to bubble on top.

- Remove from heat.

- Stir in onions, coriander leaves and green chillies.

- Allow filling to cool.

- Divide dough into 6 portions.

- Flatten one portion into a disc 3 inches in diameter. Place a portion of filling in the centre of the disc. Fold over dough to cover filling and pinch to seal. Shape into a flat round and roll out on a floured surface into a circle 6 inches in diameter.

- Make remaining parantha in the same way.

- Roast parantha on a heated tava, for 2-3 minutes till light brown. Turn over and roast for another 2-3 minutes.

- Towards the end of the roasting process, dribble a little butter or ghee on tava along edges of parantha and apply a little on top to make it crisp.

Note: For fat free tandoori parantha, grill at 220°C (425°F) for 3-4 minutes on each side. If your grill is not graded in degrees, then grill at maximum temperature.

Accompaniments

MURGH KA ACHAAR

Chicken Pickle

1 kg boneless chicken, cut into 3" cubes
200 gm (scant 1 cup) mustard oil
½ tsp asafoetida (hing)
6-8 pungent dry red chillies
1½ tsp fenugreek seeds (methi)
6-7 black cardamoms
6-7 piece cinnamon, 1" each
6-7 black peppercorns
1½ tsp chilli powder
1½ tsp salt
400 gm (3 large) onions, sliced
50 gm garlic (3 bulbs), sliced
50 gm ginger (4" piece), sliced
25 gm (10 tsp) roasted aniseed (saunf)
1½ tsp garam masala powder
1 cup vinegar

- Heat oil in a pan to smoking point.

- Reduce heat and add asafoetida. Stir and add dry red chillies and fenugreek seeds. Fry for a few seconds.

- Add whole spices, chilli powder, salt and chicken. Fry for 5 minutes stirring constantly.

- Add onions and garlic. Cover pan and cook till oil starts to bubble on top.

- Stir in ginger, aniseed, garam masala and vinegar.

- Bring to boil. Remove from heat immediately.
- Cool and bottle.

Note: Preferably, keep the pickle in a refrigerator. It will stay for 2-3 months.

SIRKÉ KA PYAZ – 1

Pickled Onions

¼ kg small Madras or pickling onions
2 cups white vinegar
1 tsp salt
1 tsp sugar

- Peel onions. Wash and dry.
- Mix all ingredients and keep covered for 12 hours.
- Remove onions and serve with any chicken preparation.

SIRKÉ KA PYAZ – 2

Pickled Onions

¼ kg small Madras or pickling onions
2 cups white vinegar
1 tsp salt
1 tsp sugar
1 slice beetroot

- Peel onions. Wash and dry.

- Mix remaining ingredients, add onions and keep covered for 12 hours.

- Remove onions and serve with any chicken preparation.

LACHHEDAR PYAZ

Sliced Onion Relish

Makes: 2 cups

2 onions
½ small beetroot or carrot
1 tbsp finely chopped mint
1 tbsp finely chopped coriander leaves
¼ tsp salt
Juice of 1 large lime

- Slice onion and beetroot or carrot very finely.

- Soak onion slices in iced water for 20 minutes. Remove and drain.

- Toss in remaining ingredients.

- Serve with barbecued chicken, kabab and biryani.

KACHUMBER

Onion and Tomato Salad

1 onion, chopped
1 cucumber, chopped
1 small carrot, chopped
1 large tomato, chopped
2 tbsp chopped coriander leaves
1 green chilli, chopped
½ tsp salt
Juice of 1 large lime

- Mix all ingredients.
- Serve with biryani.

ANNANAS RAITA

Pineapple in Spiced Curd

½ kg (2¼ cups) curd, beaten till smooth
1 cup diced pineapple
1 tbsp chopped mint leaves
½ tsp salt
½ tsp powdered black pepper

Garnish:

½ tsp roasted caraway seeds, ground
A sprig of mint

- Mix together all ingredients.
- Sprinkle over ground caraway seeds and garnish with a sprig of mint.
- Chill.
- Serve with pulao and biryani.

HARA DHANIA AUR NARIAL KI CHUTNEY

Coriander and Coconut Chutney

Makes: About 2 cups

3 cups chopped coriander leaves
1 medium-sized fresh coconut, grated
1 tbsp roasted cumin seeds
1 tbsp roasted groundnuts
6 green chillies, chopped
2 tbsp sugar
½ tbsp salt
Juice of 2 limes

- Wash coriander leaves and green chillies and pat dry.
- Mix all ingredients and grind to a paste.
- This chutney can be frozen for months.

PUDINA CHUTNEY

Mint Chutney

Makes: About 1 cup

This chutney mixed with little curd is a delicious accompaniment for tandoori tikka and kabab.

1 cup mint leaves
½ cup chopped coriander leaves
1 onion
½ tsp crushed garlic
2 chillies, chopped
½ tsp sugar or 1 tsp jaggery
½ tsp salt
1 tsp fresh lime juice
1 tsp dry pomegranate seeds (anar dana)

- Wash mint and coriander leaves and pat dry.
- Grind all ingredients to a smooth paste.
- Store in an airtight jar and preserve in a refrigerator.
- This chutney will stay for one week in a refrigerator.

PUDINA AKHROAT CHUTNEY

Mint and Walnut Chutney

Makes: About ¾ cup

½ cup chopped walnuts
4 tbsp mint leaves
½ cup thick curd, beaten till smooth
1 tsp chilli powder
¼ tsp salt

- Blend walnuts, mint leaves and ¼ cup curd in a liquidizer or food processor.
- Add remaining ingredients, mix well and serve.

MIRCHI CHA THECHA

Green Chilli Chutney – Kolhapur Style

Makes: About 1 cup

50 gm small pungent green chillies, chopped
1 tbsp oil
1 onion, grated
2 tbsp crushed garlic
1 tbsp grated coconut
1 tbsp chopped coriander leaves
½ tsp salt

- Heat 2 teaspoons oil in a pan and fry onions till light brown. Remove onion from pan, drain and keep aside.

- Add remaining oil to pan and fry green chillies lightly. Cool and grind.

- Add chillies and garlic to onion. Mix in coconut, coriander leaves and salt.

KOLHAPURI CHUTNEY

Red Chilli Chutney – Kolhapur Style

1 cup chopped coriander leaves
4 tbsp oil
2 onions, chopped
75 gm garlic
75 gm grated dry coconut
1 kg Sankeshwari, Bedgi, Reshampati, or any other very hot chillies

- Wash coriander leaves and pat dry.

- Heat a little oil at a time in a non-stick frying pan and stir-fry individually onions, garlic, coconut and coriander leaves. Allow all ingredients to cool.

- Mix fried ingredients with chillies and grind to a powder.

- Store powder in an airtight jar. This will stay for months.

TOMATO CHUTNEY – BENGAL STYLE

½ kg (6 large) tomatoes, finely chopped
1 tbsp oil
2 dried red chillies
1 tsp musterd seeds
15 sultanas (kishmish)
8 dates, stoned
1 tsp salt
½ cup sugar

Dry roast and grind to a fine powder:
½ tsp fenugreek seeds (methi)
½ tsp aniseed (saunf)
½ tsp cinnamon sticks
½ tsp seeds of green cardamom
1 bay leaf

- Heat oil in a non stick pan and add red chillies and mustard seeds. Fry for a few moments.

- Stir in tomatoes, sultanas, dates, salt and sugar. Cook till the mixture attains a smooth texture.

- Sprinkle over powdered spices and serve.

LACHHEDAR PUDINA PARANTHA

Mint Parantha

Makes: 12-14

Dough:

½ kg flour (maida)
1 tbsp ghee
½ tsp salt
1 cup chopped mint leaves

Lining:

2 tbsp ghee
2 tbsp flour (maida)

- Mix all ingredients for dough with enough water and knead into a soft dough.

- Cover dough with a damp cloth and leave for one hour.

- Heat 2 tablespoons ghee for lining in a pan and fry flour till it becomes a pale gold paste.

- Allow lining paste to cool.

- Divide dough into 12-14 portions.

- Roll out each portion into a thin roti. Spread some of the lining over roti.

- Roll roti into a sausage and roll sausage into a pin-wheel making sure to keep the folded edges on the outer side.

- Place pin-wheel flat on a floured board and roll into a thick roti.

- Roast in a regular clay or gas tandoor, or bake in an oven at 220°C (425°F) for 5 minutes.

TANDOORI ROTI

Makes: 10

¼ kg whole wheat flour (atta)
¼ tsp salt

- Mix flour and salt with a little water and knead into soft dough. Cover with a damp cloth and leave for one hour.

- Divide dough into 10 portions.

- Roll out each portion into a thick roti.

- Bake in a regular clay or gas tandoor, or in an electric oven at 220°C (425°F) for 5 minutes.

Note: Try to use a minimum quantity of flour while rolling the roti.

ROOMALI ROTI

Makes: 20-24 medium-sized roti

The word *roomali* means handkerchief. The roti is soft and pliable, just like a handkerchief and is as light as a feather. Roomali roti is an excellent accompaniment with all varieties of barbecued boneless meats and kababs.

1 kg flour (maida)
150 gm (¾ cup) Semolina
½ cup oil
1½ cups milk
1 tsp salt
1½ cups water

- Mix together all ingredients except water. Adding a little water at a time, knead into a soft dough.

- Cover with a damp cloth and leave for one hour.

- Divide dough into small portions and roll each into a paper-thin roti.

- Place an inverted tava or girdle on heat. When tava is hot, place a roti on it.

- Roast for 2 minutes. As soon as bubbles appear on the surface, turn roti and cook for a minute longer. The roti should be soft.

- Fold into four and serve immediately.

Note: Roomali roti can also be covered with a foil to keep it warm, as it becomes dry and leathery when cold.

PLAIN PULAO

1 cup basmati rice
3 tbsp oil
1" piece cinnamon
2 black cardamoms
2 cloves
1 bay leaf (tej patta)
1 tsp salt
¼ tsp turmeric powder
2 cups chicken stock or water

- Wash rice and soak in water for 20 minutes. Drain.

- Heat oil in a non-stick pan and lightly fry cinnamon, cardamom, cloves and bay leaf.

- Reduce heat and add rice, turmeric powder and salt. Fry for 8-9 minutes.

- Transfer rice into a deep pan, add chicken stock or water. Cover pan and simmer on minimum heat till rice is tender and dry.

- Discard whole spices and bay leaf, if desired, before serving.

BROWN RICE

2 cups jirga or basmati rice
3-4 tbsp oil
2 onions, sliced
1½ tbsp sugar
1 tsp cumin seeds
2-3 cloves
2-3 green cardamoms
2 pieces cinnamon, 1" each
1½ tsp salt

- Wash rice and drain.

- Heat oil in deep pan and fry onions till golden. Remove onions from pan, drain and keep aside.

- Add sugar to pan and cook on low heat for a few seconds till light brown.

- Stir in cumin seeds and whole spices and fry for one minute.

- Add fried onions, 3½ cups water and salt. Bring to boil and add rice.

- Lower heat, cover pan and simmer till rice is tender and dry.

Glossary

ENGLISH	HINDI
Almond	Badam
Aniseed	Saunf
Apricot	Khurmani
Asafoetida	Hing
Baking soda	Meetha soda
Basil leaf	Tulsi patta
Bay leaf	Tej patta
Bengal gram	Chané ki dal
Black beans-husked	Dhuli urud ki dal
Black cardamom	Badi elaichi
Black cumin seeds	Shahi jeera
Black pepper	Kali mirch
Black peppercorn	Sabut kali mirch
Black salt	Kala namak
Brain	Bheja
Bread	Double roti
Butter	Makhan
Butter-clarified	Ghee
Caraway seeds	Shahi jeera
Carrot	Gaajar
Cashew nut	Kaju
Cauliflower	Phool gobi
Chicken	Murgh
Chickpeas	Sufaid chana

ENGLISH	HINDI
Chironji	Chironji / charoli
Cinnamon	Dalchini
Clove	Laung
Coconut	Nariyal
Coconut-dried	Copra
Coriander-fresh	Hara dhania
Coriander-seeds	Sabut dhania
Corn	Makkai
Cottage cheese	Paneer
Cream	Cream
Cucumber	Kheera
Cucumber seeds	Kheeré ké beej
Cumin seeds	Jeera
Curd	Dahi
Curry leaf	Kari patta
Date	Khajoor
Dill	Sua bhaji
Egg	Anda
Fennel	Saunf
Fenugreek leaves	Methi
Fenugreek leaves-dried	Kasuri methi
Fenugreek seeds	Methi dana
Fig	Anjeer
Fish	Machchi
Flour	Maida
Garlic	Lehsun
Ginger-dried	Sonth
Ginger-fresh	Adrak
Gram flour	Besan
Gram-green	Hara chana
Gram-roasted	Bhuné chané
Green cardamom	Chhoti elaichi
Green chilli	Hari mirch
Green capsicum	Shimla mirch
Green peas	Matar
Honey	Madh / Shahad
Horse radish	Sufaid mooli
Jaggery	Gur

ENGLISH	HINDI
Kidney	Gurda
Kidney beans	Rajmah
Lentils	Dal
Lettuce	Salad ke patté
Lime	Neebu
Liver	Kaleji
Mace	Javitri
Mango	Aam
Mango-raw, dried, powdered	Pisa amchur
Mango-raw, dried	Sabut amchur
Marsh melon seeds	Kharbooze ké beej
Milk	Doodh
Milk condensed-unsweetened	Khoya
Mince	Keema
Mint	Pudina
Mustard oil	Sarson ka tel
Mustard seeds	Rai
Mustard seeds-yellow	Peeli sarson
Mutton	Gosht
Nutmeg	Jaiphal
Onion seeds	Kalaunji
Onion	Pyaz
Orange	Santra
Papaya-raw	Kaccha papeeta
Pickle	Achaar
Pigeon peas	Arhar ki dal (Toover)
Pineapple	Annanas
Pistachio nuts	Pista
Pomegranate seeds	Anar dana
Poppy seeds	Khus khus
Potato	Alu
Red capsicum	Lal Shimla mirch
Red chilli-powder	Pisi hui lal mirch
Red chilli-whole	Sabut lal mirch
Rice	Chawal
Rock salt	Lohori namak
Rose water	Gulabjal
Saffron	Kesar / Zafran

ENGLISH	HINDI
Salt	Namak
Screwpine flower essence	Kewra
Semolina	Sooji / Rava
Sesame oil	Til ka tel
Sesame seeds	Sufaid til
Silver leaf	Chandi ka varak
Spinach	Palak
Star anise	Badiyan
Sugar	Cheeni
Sugar candy	Misri
Sultana	Kishmish
Tamarind	Imli
Thyme	Ajwain
Tomato	Tamatar
Top of milk	Malai/balai
Turmeric	Haldi
Vinegar	Sirka
Walnut	Akhroat
Watermelon seeds	Tarbooz ke beej
Wheat	Gehun
Whole wheat flour	Atta
Yoghurt	Substitute for dahi

Char Magaz:
A mixture of water melon, marsh melon, cucumber and pumpkin seeds.

Kokum:
A dry sour plum – the botanical name is *Garcina Indica*.

Index

- Kashmiri murgh - goshtaba masala(Chicken meatballs in curd gravy) 109
- Kashmiri murgh rogan josh (Chicken in tomato and curd gravy) 107
- Yakhani Kashmiri murgh (Chicken curry) 105

Kerala Specialities:
- Kozhi curry (Chicken curry- Malabar style) 188
- Kozhi erachi paal curry (Chicken in coconut curry - Kerala style) 186
- Kozhi istu (Chicken and vegetable curry - Kerala style) 192
- Kozhi varattiyathu (Chicken masala - Malabar style) 190

Kofta:
- Kashmiri murgh - goshtaba masala (Chicken meatballs in curd gravy - Kashmir style) 109
- Murgh kofta (Chicken meatball curry) 97
- Nargisi murgh kofta curry (Scotch eggs - Mughlai style) 102
- Shikampuri murgh kofta (Stuffed chicken meatball curry) 99

Konkani Specialities:
- Kairee chi kombri (Chicken curry) 178
- Kombri cha salna (Chicken in crab masala) 176
- Naral chi kombri - 1(Chicken curry) 174
- Naral chi kombri - 2 (Chicken curry) 175

- Murgh Noorjehani (Chicken with curd and nuts) 84
- Murgh rogan josh (Chicken in tomato and curd gravy) 92
- Murgh zalfrazie (Chicken curry laced with eggs) 94
- Nargisi murgh kofta curry (Scotch eggs) 102
- Pista murgh (Chicken with pistachio nuts) 75
- Sandli murgh (Saffron flavoured chicken) 88
- Shikampuri murgh kofta (Stuffed chicken meatball curry) 99
- Zafrani bharwa murgh (Saffron flavoured stuffed chicken) 65

Pahadi Specialities:
- Pahadi chhaach murgh (Chicken in curd - Chamba style) 130
- Pahadi khatti kukardi (Chicken in sour gravy - Kangra style) 126
- Pahadi madra murgh (Chicken with curd - Kangra style) 128

Parsi Specialities:
- Aleti paleti (Savoury chicken liver and gizzard) 159
- Kaju ma murghi (Chicken with cashew nuts) 154
- Murghi na farcha (Fried chicken) 151
- Murghi nu dhansakh (Chicken with lentils and vegetables) 156
- Sali ma murghi (Chicken with straw potatoes) 152

Punjabi Specialities:
- Hara chana murgh (Chicken with fresh green gram) 122

- Kadahi murgh (Fried chicken in tomato gravy) 114
- Kali mirch murgh (Chicken curry with black pepper) 112
- Murgh keema matar (Minced chicken with green peas) 124
- Murgh methi (Chicken with fenugreek) 118
- Murgh palak (Chicken with spinach) 116
- Sabz murgh (Chicken in green herbs) 120

Rajasthani Specialities:
- Khad murgh keema (Baked chicken mince) 138
- Murgh makkai (Chicken with corn) 136
- Rajasthani lal murgh (Chicken in red gravy) 141
- Rajasthani sufaid murgh (White chicken curry) 140

Sindhi Specialities:
- Seyal murgh (Chicken curry with onions and green herbs) 143
- Sindhi elaichi murgh (Cardamom flavoured chicken) 145
- Sindhi hara murgh (Chicken in green curry) 146
- Sindhi methi murgh (Chicken with fenugreek leaves) 147

Tamil Specialities:
- Kozhi Chettinad (Chicken fry - Chettinad style) 184
- Kozhi kuzhumbu (Chicken curry - Madras style) 180
- Kozhi varatha kosambu (Chicken Chettinad) 182

Whole Chicken:
- Murgh musallam (Whole masala chicken) 63

- Zafrani bharwa murgh (Saffron flavoured stuffed chicken) 65

RICE
Biryani:
- Biryani Shahjehani (Chicken biryani - Mughlai style) 210
- Bohri murgh biryani (Chicken biryani - Bohra style) 215
- Dumpukht murgh biryani (Chicken biryani) 208
- Kacché murgh ki biryani (Chicken biryani) 213
- Kozhi biryani (Chicken biryani - Malabar style) 217

Pulao:
- Goan kombi pulao (Chicken pulao - Goa style) 200
- Golyacha murgh pulao (Chicken meatball pulao) 203
- Komri pulao (Chicken and coconut pulao - Konkan style) 201
- Murgh pulao (Chicken pulao) 198
- Murgh tikka pulao (Barbecued chicken pulao) 206

ROTI
Keema naan (Naan stuffed with chicken mince) 221
Keema parantha (Parantha stuffed with chicken mince) 224

SALADS
Chatpata murgh salad (Tangy chicken salad) 6
Murgh aur makkai salad (Chicken and corn salad with vinaigrette dressing) 8
Murgh aur rajmah salad (Chicken and kidney bean

Tandoori murgh pakora (Tandoori chicken fritters) 25

Tikka:
- Achari murgh tikka (Barbecued pickled chicken) 15
- Haryali murgh tikka (Barbecued chicken in green
    herbs) 11
- Murgh malai tikka (Grilled creamy chicken) 13